# Cambridge Elements ≡

Elements in Politics and Society in Latin America
edited by
Maria Victoria Murillo
*Columbia University*
Juan Pablo Luna
*The Pontifical Catholic University of Chile*
Andrew Schrank
*Brown University*

# PARTIES AND NEW TECHNOLOGIES IN LATIN AMERICA

Rafael Piñeiro-Rodríguez
*Universidad Católica del Uruguay*

Fernando Rosenblatt
*The University of Manchester*

Gabriel Vommaro
*Universidad Nacional de San Martín/CONICET*

Laura Wills-Otero
*Universidad de los Andes*

CAMBRIDGE
UNIVERSITY PRESS

# CAMBRIDGE
## UNIVERSITY PRESS

Shaftesbury Road, Cambridge CB2 8EA, United Kingdom

One Liberty Plaza, 20th Floor, New York, NY 10006, USA

477 Williamstown Road, Port Melbourne, VIC 3207, Australia

314–321, 3rd Floor, Plot 3, Splendor Forum, Jasola District Centre,
New Delhi – 110025, India

103 Penang Road, #05–06/07, Visioncrest Commercial, Singapore 238467

Cambridge University Press is part of Cambridge University Press & Assessment,
a department of the University of Cambridge.

We share the University's mission to contribute to society through the pursuit
of education, learning and research at the highest international levels of excellence.

www.cambridge.org
Information on this title: www.cambridge.org/9781009623049

DOI: 10.1017/9781009623018

First published 2024

*A catalogue record for this publication is available from the British Library*

ISBN 978-1-009-62304-9 Hardback
ISBN 978-1-009-62302-5 Paperback
ISSN 2515-5253 (online)
ISSN 2515-5245 (print)

Cambridge University Press & Assessment has no responsibility for the persistence
or accuracy of URLs for external or third-party internet websites referred to in this
publication and does not guarantee that any content on such websites is, or will
remain, accurate or appropriate.

# Parties and New Technologies in Latin America

Elements in Politics and Society in Latin America

DOI: 10.1017/9781009623018
First published online: December 2024

Rafael Piñeiro-Rodríguez
*Universidad Católica del Uruguay*

Fernando Rosenblatt
*The University of Manchester*

Gabriel Vommaro
*Universidad Nacional de San Martín/CONICET*

Laura Wills-Otero
*Universidad de los Andes*

**Author for correspondence:** Fernando Rosenblatt,
fernando.rosenblatt@manchester.ac.uk

**Abstract:** This Element analyzes the incorporation of new information and communication technologies (ICTs) by different parties in Latin America to organize volunteers and mobilize supporters during elections. It assesses ICT-related changes in how parties recruit prospective candidates, collect information about citizens' preferences, and mobilize for elections and how these changes have reduced the power of the rank and file within party organizations. Party leaders have an incentive to incorporate new ICTs to increase electoral efficacy and reduce the role of rank-and-file members in performing essential party functions. However, the result of the incorporation of technology depends on leaders' capacity to control the process within the party. Based on case studies of ICT incorporation by various Latin American parties and electoral campaigns, the authors posit that the incorporation of technology will consolidate a power dynamic that predates the adoption of ICTs to fulfill organizational functions.

**Keywords:** information and communication technologies, Latin America, party organizations, activism, electoral campaigns

ISBNs: 9781009623049 (HB), 9781009623025 (PB), 9781009623018 (OC)
ISSNs: 2515-5253 (online), 2515-5245 (print)

# Contents

# Introduction

Party organizations are in decline in many parts of the world (Dalton and Wattenberg 2000; Dalton, McAllister, and Wattenberg 2000; Dalton and Weldon 2007; Mainwaring 2018). In Latin America, this decline is a pervasive problem because it interacts with fragile democracies and structural challenges (i.e. inequality, poverty, and informality) (Kitschelt et al. 2010; Luna 2014; Mainwaring 2018; Mainwaring and Zoco 2007; Roberts 2014; Van Dyck 2017). Since the Third Wave of democratization, Latin America has witnessed the emergence of numerous parties that have been unable to survive and take root in society (Levitsky, Loxton, and Van Dyck 2016). Moreover, many of these new parties fail to perform the basic functions of democratic representation, that is, the aggregation of societal interests and the coordination among ambitious politicians (Luna et al. 2021). In this context, new information and communication technologies (ICTs) afford emerging political actors an opportunity to rapidly build an electoral vehicle and afford established political leaders the means to transform party organizations.

There exists a rich literature on the incorporation of new ICTs in political parties, but most studies to date have analyzed the effects in the United States and European countries, highly developed societies that have institutionalized party organizations and strong political institutions. Studying the political parties' incorporation of new ICTs in Latin America affords an opportunity to examine the phenomenon in a very different context, namely, developing societies with weak institutions and generally weak organizational development of parties. In Latin America, in the absence of strong organizations, the incorporation of new ICTs provides an opportunity for leaders to circumvent the development of organizational structures to mobilize voters or to transform existing weak organizational structures.

In a context of weakly organized parties or nonexistent party organizations, Latin American cases show the potential and the limits of new ICTs to replace the work of people in organizing complex and sustained collective action. New ICTs can engage people in the public realm and even improve their capacity for collective action. However, this is neither an automatic process nor the unequivocal result of the incorporation of new ICTs in politics. People can now more easily be activated for electoral campaigning. However, at the same time, the weakening of organizational structures that foster sustained collective action might weaken people's voice within party organizations and might prevent the organizational development of new parties.

Although internet penetration in Latin America does not yet reach the levels observed in the US, for most people in the region the internet has become a "mundane tool," (Nielsen 2011) especially in the last decade (Robinson et al. 2020). There is widespread internet penetration in the region; in the most developed countries, more than 75 percent of the population has internet access, and in some countries access reaches 90 percent (see Table 1). WhatsApp and Facebook are the most widely used social media platforms with around 50 percent of the population having access to one or both of these platforms. The marked growth of the use of the internet in the region and the prolific generation of personal data led campaigns and candidates to consider how they might use new ICTs for political purposes. The incorporation of new ICTs was not only attractive because of their widespread use and increased affordability, but also because they enabled candidates and parties to reach and mobilize voters and constituencies more easily.

**Table 1** Internet access and new ICT users in Latin America (percentage of the population).

| Country | Internet | WhatsApp | Facebook | X (Twitter) | TikTok |
|---|---|---|---|---|---|
| Argentina | 88.4 | 53.0 | 59.2 | 16.3 | 35.1 |
| Bolivia | 66.0 | 30.0 | 58.1 | 5.0 | NA |
| Brazil | 80.5 | 64.7 | 50.7 | 11.3 | 38.2 |
| Chile | 90.2[*] | 56.5 | 62.0 | 18.6 | 57.4 |
| Colombia | 72.8 | 55.7 | 64.6 | 10.8 | 38.8 |
| Costa Rica | 82.6 | 52.9 | 60.8 | 13.1 | NA |
| Dominican Republic | 85.2[*] | 39.7 | 46.3 | 7.6 | NA |
| Ecuador | 69.7 | 41.2 | 66.7 | 10.0 | 53.6 |
| El Salvador | 62.9[*] | 53.0 | 56.8 | 11.2 | NA |
| Guatemala | 50.8[*] | 44.5 | 45.8 | 5.2 | NA |
| Honduras | 48.1[*] | 39.3 | 37.9 | 4.9 | NA |
| Mexico | 75.6[*] | 54.7 | 65.4 | 13.5 | 45.1 |
| Nicaragua | 57.1[*] | 36.4 | 46.8 | 3.9 | NA |
| Panama | 67.5[*] | 53.0 | 39.7 | 14.6 | NA |
| Paraguay | 76.3 | 50.1 | 51.6 | 10.7 | NA |
| Peru | 74.7 | 47.2 | 67.1 | 8.1 | 49.5 |
| Uruguay | 89.9 | 55.7 | 58.4 | 20.5 | 43.5 |
| Venezuela | NA | 39.8 | 42.0 | 6.7 | NA |

**Sources:** Internet access, World Development Indicators (World Bank); WhatsApp, Facebook, X, and TikTok users, World Population Review.
**Notes:** Percentage of the population with access to internet in 2022, * indicates access in 2021. WhatsApp users in 2021; Facebook, X, and TikTok users in 2023.

Technology has dramatically changed social and political interactions. The most important shock introduced by the new ICT revolution is the dramatic reduction in the cost of information and communication. In politics, new ICTs can be used in different ways for political campaigns and by parties. In principle, technological innovations have reduced the costs of contacting and engaging people with politics (Bennett and Segerberg 2013). New ICTs have dramatically changed how candidates, parties, and social organizations communicate with citizens (Epstein 2018; Gainous and Wagner 2014; Gibson 2020; Issenberg 2012; Karpf 2016). However, new ICTs have not only affected how political actors communicate with people but have also changed how people organize themselves to pursue political goals (Bennett and Segerberg 2013; Bimber 2003; Epstein 2018; Gibson 2015, 2020; Karpf 2012; Vaccari and Valeriani 2016, among others).

We use the term "new ICTs" to denote a set of complementary computer-based tools that constitute a technological package or cluster. This cluster entails, for example: instant messaging apps (e.g. WhatsApp or Telegram); software to integrate administrative data with individuals' personal data to develop field operations (e.g. variations of Customer Relationship Management – CRM – platforms, and reports of electoral results and other administrative data at the lowest level available – in some cases census tracks); social listening tools (e.g. tailored and standard dashboards and reports of the conversation on X); and tools for targeting campaign propaganda on social networks and on other internet-based platforms (e.g. Google ads, Facebook ads, Facebook A/B testing, and Meta Pixel). These technologies, associated with the growth of the internet and the reduction in the cost of data-processing by computers, facilitate personalized communication and the capacity to collect, analyze, and manage large amounts of data.

This cluster of new ICTs constitutes the foundation of what Epstein (2018) calls a political communication revolution. In the US, this revolution has produced a new political communication order (PCO), that is, the Information PCO. In Latin America, not all political actors have adopted these new ICTs as their primary means of political communication. Thus, the region is in transition and new ICTs have not yet become the established PCO. Nonetheless, as new ICTs have become more widespread and as the costs of such tools have dramatically decreased in the last decade, some political actors in the region have incorporated new ICTs in various ways, giving rise to a hybrid media system (Chadwick 2017), that is, a system in which digital media coexist with traditional media. Latin American parties and candidates are latecomers to the new ICT revolution. In this sense, they have not undergone the phases in the digital campaigning cycle described by Gibson (2020) for Australia, France, the UK, and the US (experimentation, standardization and professionalization, community building and activist mobilization, and individual voter mobilization). Latin American parties combined these different phases (especially in terms of tools and communication modes).

In a given political communication revolution and in the resulting PCO (Epstein 2018), parties typically differ in the ways they use new ICTs. While Epstein (2018) seeks to explain how PCOs change, we focus on how such changes materialize in different dimensions in diverse party organizations and electoral vehicles. Technology affects the way people engage with political organizations and, in turn, their role within such organizations. New ICTs can affect the power of people within organizations in various ways (Gerbaudo 2021; Gibson 2020; Stromer-Galley 2019; Tufekci 2017). For example, technology can empower people within organizations by boosting their capacity to organize themselves more efficiently or disempower them by replacing organizers. While the empowerment of people within organizations contributes to democratic responsiveness, the disempowerment of organizers facilitates the concentration of power in the hands of an organization's leaders.

The main novelty of new ICTs in terms of their effect on collective action is that they allow people to engage individually with social and political organizations. These new technologies facilitate a massive one-to-one linkage between the organization and each member. In the past, engaging people in an organization was only possible through collective engagement; that is, becoming part of a group. New ICTs have eliminated the need for intermediate organizational structures to convene people to work for a given collective action. Engaging members in an atomized way (i.e. individual engagement) precludes them from coordinating with other members to keep leaders accountable or to have a voice in the organization's decision-making. Thus, individual engagement prevents the transformation of members into stakeholders within the organization. Therefore, the effect of new ICTs depends on whether organizations use technology to promote collective or individual engagement.

The diffusion or concentration of power within social and political organizations engendered by technological change affects the functioning of democracy. Organizations are democratic when their leaders are responsive to their fellow members and in order for leaders to remain responsive, members need to be able to hold them accountable on a permanent basis (in elections and between elections). The concentration of power, in turn, makes organizations less democratic and more dependent on the fate of their leaders. Therefore, technology affects the nature of the organizations through which citizens engage in politics by affecting organizations' ability to remain stable vehicles that can channel citizens' preferences. Moreover, leaders and personalistic vehicles that almost exclusively rely on new ICTs for electoral mobilization exacerbate their organizational weakness and become more fragile in the face of electoral defeats or other setbacks. New ICTs might favor the electoral growth of new electoral vehicles and opportunistic leaders who capture the social mood, but then have difficulties both coordinating among their leaders and aggregating social interests (Luna et al. 2021).

Party structures based on the organization of people fulfill multiple functions for the reproduction of political parties. Aldrich (1995) defines parties as institutions that solve collective action, public choice, and social choice problems. We focus on the role of parties as organizations that solve collective action challenges in elections. First, organizational structures recruit prospective leaders and candidates. Second, they communicate citizens' preferences to party leaders. Third, they organize and mobilize people in the field for electoral campaigns. New ICTs, which facilitate personalized communication and enhance the capacity to collect, analyze, and manage large amounts of data, can empower or substitute for – and therefore diminish – the role people and organizational structures play in performing these party functions.

New ICTs have facilitated contacting prospective volunteers and made it easier for supporters to engage with an electoral campaign. In Latin America, some new parties that were created by successful leaders at the national level or by those who have been successful in one or a few regions use new ICTs to recruit new leaders and candidates at the local level throughout the country. The advancement of tools for social inquiry (e.g. social listening through social networks) gave parties additional and affordable ways to capture citizens' preferences. The possibility of reaching voters and prospective volunteers at a low cost and the availability of microtargeting strategies have significantly increased politicians' interest in including new ICTs in their campaigns (Issenberg 2012).

This Element analyzes the incorporation of technology to fulfill the three main party functions (i.e. recruiting candidates, collecting citizens' preferences, and mobilizing and organizing members) by different party organizations and electoral vehicles in Latin America. New ICTs have various impacts on democracy. They have significantly influenced how people become informed about politics. In this regard, there is a vast literature on misinformation, disinformation, and "fake news" and its strategic use in elections (Benkler, Faris, and Roberts 2018; Bennett and Livingston 2020; Guess and Lyons 2020). There is also a vast literature on how social media has affected the way politicians reach voters (Aldrich et al. 2016; Bene 2017; Enli and Skogerbø 2013; Jacobs and Spierings 2019; Luna et al. 2022; Schmuck and Hameleers 2020). Nonetheless, this Element only refers to these issues when they are connected to our main concern about the role new ICTs play in the organization of collective action and the fulfillment of parties' main functions. In this Element, we characterize the technological environment that conditions the availability of new ICTs in Latin America and then focus on the process that leads to the different organizational outcomes.

In the next section, we outline our theoretical framework. Our theory seeks to account for the process of incorporating new ICTs to perform essential party functions and the outcome of this incorporation in terms of the distribution of power within party organizations. We posit that incorporating technology in parties is a two-stage process. It involves, first, an exogenous stage, essentially determined by: the characteristics of the electorate and the electoral competition that affect the efficacy of new ICTs as campaign tools; the affordability of technology; the institutional setting that governs campaign finance rules, the rules that limit the use of existing databases containing personal data, and the rules that govern data-gathering for electoral purposes. The second stage involves an endogenous process that is determined by leaders' decisions to incorporate technology in interaction with the stakeholders of the organizational structure. The incorporation of technology within a party is thus ultimately determined by the dynamics of the endogenous process related to the main traits of the organization (Raniolo, Tarditi, and Vittori 2021). Party leaders are the ones who decide whether and how to adopt new ICTs based on exogenous conditions. However, their capacity to control the process will determine the degree and characteristics of the technological incorporation.

The process of incorporating new ICTs can result in three different organizational outcomes: an ersatz organization, a hybrid, or an empowered organization. Ersatz organizations result when leaders do not face a dense and/or complex organization and thus have no constraints on incorporating new ICTs. As a result, new ICTs replace the role of people in organizations. These are ersatz organizations because technology is limited in its ability to serve as a functional equivalent for the work people do in traditional organizations. For example, regarding the selection of candidates and horizontal coordination among candidates, technology provides neither the rules nor the socialization process to coordinate in office. Regarding the collection of citizens' preferences, technology reduces the activists' capacity to influence party decision-making. Finally, regarding the mobilization and organization of voters, technology still depends on organizers to coordinate complex collective action in the field. It also engages people individually, precluding the possibility of transforming them into party stakeholders.

When leaders face a dense and/or complex organization, the result can be a hybrid or an empowered organization. In the former, new ICTs partially substitute for the role of people in fulfilling some party functions. In the latter, the incorporation of new ICTs boosts organization members' capacity to perform party functions.

In the second section, we describe the supply side of new ICTs for political campaigning and mobilization in the region based on in-depth interviews with service providers and consultants in Argentina, Chile, Colombia, Costa Rica, and Uruguay who specialize in the political applications of new ICTs. We also complement the supply-side picture with the demand-side perspective based on in-depth interviews with politicians in these countries.

The third section includes an illustration of the theory based on different cases in Latin America. The cases included in this Element exhibit the greatest possible variance in terms of organizational structure, a crucial independent variable in our theoretical framework. Nevertheless, the cases studied in this Element were selected based on their heuristic value (George and Bennett 2005). All are cases of incorporation of new ICTs that allow us to "inductively identify new variables, hypotheses, causal mechanisms, and causal paths" (George and Bennett 2005, 75). Although in this Element we focus on countries with high levels of socioeconomic development in the Latin American context, as shown in Table 1, internet penetration and the use of new ICTs are relatively homogeneous across the region (except for Bolivia and some Central American countries).

We describe the case of the Argentinean Propuesta Republicana (Republican Proposal, PRO) party to illustrate how new ICTs make it possible to engage supporters in campaigns without making them party stakeholders. This individual engagement allows PRO leaders to activate supporters without endangering the leaders' control of the party. We then analyze the case of Rodolfo Hernández and his electoral vehicle, Liga de Gobernantes Anticorrupción (Anti-Corruption Rulers' League, LIGA), in Colombia to show how ICTs cannot obviate the need for organizers to undertake complex collective actions in campaigns. We then consider the case of the Lista del Pueblo (People's List, LdP) in Chile to show how new ICTs can facilitate fast coordination for electoral campaigns to achieve electoral success, though they are insufficient to organize sustained collective action once a party comes into office. We also analyze the cases of the Frente Amplio (Broad Front, FA) and the Partido Nacional (National Party, PN) in Uruguay, where we show the tensions that the incorporation of new ICTs can produce between the national party elite and local leaders or activists in established party organizations.

Finally, we conclude our study by analyzing how organizational structures condition the incorporation of new ICTs, the degree to which technology can replace people in the performance of essential party functions, and the concomitant effect of these potential changes on power distribution within parties.

## Theory

There is a vast literature covering the US and, especially, Europe, that surveys the incorporation of new ICTs in political parties and how new ICTs have engendered organizational changes and innovations (e.g. the emergence of platform parties). Part of this literature describes the differences and similarities in the incorporation of new ICTs across parties (Barberà et al. 2021; González-Cacheda and Cancela Outeda 2024) and elites' preferences for incorporating these new technologies (Dommett 2020). Other authors survey the incorporation of new ICTs to engage members with the party and include them in the decision-making processes (Biancalana and Vittori 2021, 2023; De Blasio and Viviani 2020; Gibson, Greffet, and Cantijoch 2017; Gomez and Ramiro 2019; Raniolo, Tarditi, and Vittori 2021). There is general agreement within this literature that ICT incorporation, while it exhibits some variation (especially between newer and older parties), is largely homogeneous across developed countries and it does not necessarily produce an internal democratizing effect.

New ICTs have reduced the cost of mobilization and have thus facilitated political action. Karpf (2012) claims that lowered costs "have made individual political actions far easier. Changes in communications technology alter one set of organizing constraints by dramatically lowering the marginal cost of communication" (7–8). Moreover, Bennett and Segerberg (2013) argue that new ICTs have transformed collective action into "connective action," which they define as a "large-scale personalized and digitally mediated political engagement" (5). While in classical collective action people's engagement is based on an organizational structure that provides the necessary resources for mobilization, connective action is based on "communication-based networks" that allow personalized, individual engagement.

From the connective action perspective, participation is enhanced by technological changes because individuals can directly engage in political action without the need for intermediating organizational structures or leaders. Vaccari and Valeriani (2016) argue that technological changes have empowered citizens and flattened organizational hierarchies. The communicative approach to collective action (Bimber, Flanagin, and Stohl 2012) focuses on how technology has increased individual agency but does not problematize the organizational-level constraints on such agency, because this literature assumes that formal organizations are not necessary for collective action. While this approach can describe and explain ephemeral instances of collective action, it cannot account for more complex and sustained forms of it.

Complex political action requires a clearly defined division of labor to carry out very different tasks that can only be accomplished through structured organizations. For example, an online or even an offline protest can be organized through unstructured networks. However, these same unstructured networks cannot organize complex protest actions or take part in complex and sustained negotiations. More critically, these unstructured networks lack established procedures to hold members accountable for their political actions. The main shortcoming of the communicative approach is that it considers connective action as functionally equivalent to classical forms of collective action.

The effect of new ICTs on collective action cannot be assessed by looking only at how ICTs empower individuals; rather, one must consider how ICTs are used by formal organizations to engage members in collective action. These formal and traditional organizations still have the greatest capacity to influence political processes. New ICTs offer a new way to engage people in collective action, namely, individual engagement in collective action. New ICTs facilitate a massive one-to-one linkage between the organization and each adherent. They make it possible to carry out with technology critical party functions previously performed by people. The impact of new ICTs thus will depend on whether traditional organizations use technology to empower or replace people in performing party functions and whether ICTs are used to promote collective engagement or, instead, to promote individual engagement with the organization.

Collective action in political parties is, by definition, complex and necessarily sustained (Aldrich 1995). New ICTs have introduced changes in the practices of traditional party organizations (Gibson 2020). Yet, the effects of technological innovation on collective action in party organizations cannot be explained without considering how parties use such technologies to engage people in political activities. Exerting control over the main functions of the organization is a source of power. If leaders increase their control over party functions, they concomitantly reduce other party members' roles in carrying out such functions. Hence, other party members become disposable and lose the power to challenge the leadership. Conversely, new ICTs can also boost the capacity of individuals to make collective action more efficient and more effective. Thus, when technology improves the capacity of people within organizations to organize collective action it empowers people vis-à-vis leaders.

We claim that several factors determine how parties incorporate new ICTs, including the characteristics of a party's electorate and the electoral competition that affect the efficacy of new ICTs as campaign tools, the affordability of technology, the institutional setting, leaders' decisions, and the attributes of existing organizational structures. The interaction between these factors determines whether and how parties incorporate technology to perform three basic organizational functions of parties, namely the recruitment of prospective leaders and candidates; the collection of information about citizens' concerns and preferences; and the organization and mobilization of people in the field for political campaigns. The interaction of these factors also determines how new ICTs empower or disempower people within organizations and, in turn, affect the concentration of power within parties (Gibson 2020).

## ICTs and the Functions of Parties

One of the main functions of political parties is candidate recruitment, that is, identifying and recruiting prospective leaders to run for office at different levels of government (Hazan and Rahat 2010; Siavelis and Morgenstern 2008). To succeed electorally, political parties need competitive candidates at every electoral level (national, regional, and local). Political recruitment is the process by which parties attract prospective candidates to run for office. More broadly, organizations carry out the task of recruiting and transforming adherents into leaders; that is, people committed to the goals of the organization who take responsibility for outcomes (Ganz 2009; Han 2014).

Traditionally, political parties recruit leaders and prospective candidates in different ways, depending on the nature of the party and the characteristics of the organization (e.g. its presence in the territory). For example, cadre parties recruit candidates and leaders from the local elites. Mass parties recruit vast numbers of members and then select leaders from among their most committed members. Professional electoral parties select people – not necessarily party insiders – from different spheres of society based mainly or entirely on their perceived electability. Movement parties can draw upon constituent social organizations to cultivate new leaders. All of these recruitment approaches require information about people. To obtain this information, parties usually rely on organizational structures that are more or less developed, more or less institutionalized, and more or less territorially extended. Without an organizational structure, it is hard to detect and attract prospective leaders and candidates. In turn, without local leaders and candidates, parties at the local level face the challenge of effectively mobilizing voters for local and national elections.

The challenge of recruiting candidates and expanding the organization throughout the country is daunting for new parties or outsiders who search for prospective candidates at the local or regional level. These parties and outsiders lack the knowledge or the information to identify prospective leaders and candidates and, in most cases, they do not have ties with local-level organizations to provide them with this information. New ICTs offer new parties and outsiders a solution to this challenge and offer established parties an alternative to traditional forms of obtaining information needed for candidate recruitment. When party organizations are not dense and lack the necessary networks on the ground to obtain information about prospective leaders and candidates, new ICTs offer a solution. They allow parties to contact would-be activists, leaders, and candidates, which might speed up the organization's process of territorial development and candidate recruitment.

In Latin America, some new parties founded by successful leaders at the national level or that have been successful in one or a few regions use new ICTs to recruit new leaders and candidates at the local level throughout the country. For example, in Colombia, Rodolfo Hernández was an independent candidate who ran in the 2022 presidential elections. He was mayor of the city of Bucaramanga (2016–2019) and later decided to run for the presidency without the support of any political party. Espousing typical antiestablishment rhetoric, he built a network of supporters using a computer application that encouraged users to engage new adherents in the campaign. Those who recruited more supporters acquired more recognition and increased their own chances of becoming a candidate of the Hernández movement in the subsequent local elections. However, Hernández decided not to build a national organization.

In Chile, in the context of the election of the constitutional assembly members, different lists of independent candidates emerged. One of the most prominent of these was the Lista del Pueblo (List of the People, LdP). National LdP leaders both contacted some territorial leaders and provided an online platform to recruit other interested individuals. In fact, 33 percent of LdP candidates for the constitutional assembly were recruited online (Nocetto et al. 2021). Yet, a few months after achieving electoral success, the group imploded and disappeared as a caucus within the Constitutional Convention. Also in Chile, Evolución Política (Political Evolution, Evópoli), a party founded in 2012, created a platform named "Community Leaders" to invite independent individuals to become candidates for local councils. People were encouraged to join and sign up. The process to become a prospective candidate involved different stages, most of them based on online forms and questionnaires.

In Uruguay, the Partido de la Gente (Peoples' Party), a new party whose leader, Edgardo Novick, gained fame as a businessman and ran a relatively successful campaign for the Montevideo municipality, used this strategy to recruit mayoral candidates throughout the country. The party's approach to candidate selection emulated the recruitment of executives in the private sector. Nonetheless, after performing poorly in the national election, the party did not run candidates in the local elections.

In Argentina, the PRO used new ICTs extensively to recruit activists and leaders in all parts of the country. This strategy helped the party to consolidate the organization at the local level throughout the territory. This was critical for a party that was born in the city of Buenos Aires and had difficulties expanding territorially (Vommaro 2023). Nevertheless, in those localities where the party had organization, this centralized ICT strategy sometimes engendered conflict with the local branch of the party.

Even though this strategy accomplishes the goal of supplying the demand for new leaders and candidates, it also has significant shortcomings, as the cases reviewed above illustrate. First, while recruitment via new ICTs can rapidly identify new candidates, candidates recruited in this manner do not undergo a process of socialization within the organization and are thus less reliable in terms of their loyalty to the organization, as in the case of the LdP in Chile. Second, identifying prospective leaders and candidates is only the first step in a process whereby these recruits become leaders or candidates with the capacity to develop the party organization in the territory. To achieve this goal, a party needs organizational capacity at the central level to deliver resources and to monitor and hold those new leaders accountable, as in the case of Rodolfo Hernández in Colombia. Third, the ICT approach might produce conflicts with existing local branches of the party, as in the case of the PRO in Argentina.

This strategy might entail different consequences for parties with existing functioning organizations. National leaders could be tempted to recruit candidates centrally, bypassing existing local organizational structures. For example, the PRO in Argentina did not use this strategy in places where there were established leaders for fear of igniting a conflict with those leaders. This example illustrates how the possibility of using new ICTs to centrally recruit members and candidates might affect the distribution of power between the national- and local-level authorities.

A second function of political parties is to channel and express citizens' preferences in the political arena. To achieve that goal, parties need to collect information about citizens' preferences in different ways. The traditional way parties collect information relies on their members' connections with society. Through these connections, parties incorporate citizens' and social organizations' preferences. Cadre parties resorted to their leaders' ties with local elites. Mass-based parties, born in the context of the expansion of suffrage, built more complex organizations with an active membership that developed and reproduced connections with society.

The development of tools for social inquiry (e.g. public opinion polls) gave parties additional ways to capture citizens' preferences. Professional electoral parties make extensive use of these tools and of professionals who have expertise in areas relevant to parties' electoral performance. The availability of these tools and experts partially substitutes for active members as a way to collect citizens' preferences. However, public opinion data and experts' assessments are expensive. New ICTs have reduced the costs and multiplied the potential ways of capturing citizens' preferences, thus increasing the incentives for party leaders to seek substitutes for or to downplay the role of active members. For example, online panels and social listening tools based on social network analytics provide politicians with ongoing, relatively low-cost, real-time access to information about citizens' preferences even at the local level. Also, parties and candidates collect and analyze large volumes of data that integrate public administrative information with information generated by the party (or the candidate) and data from other private sources. With this information, candidates and parties can capture the problems, needs, or interests of very specific geographic units. Before the new ICT revolution, obtaining such information was only possible by having party members in the territory.

New ICTs have thus introduced novel tools and reduced the costs of traditional tools for surveying citizens' preferences. This, in turn, has created an opportunity for new parties or emerging candidates to collect information about the electorate without the need to build an organization with roots in society (Bogliaccini et. al 2019). In Chile, for example, political parties, and especially individual candidates, use social listening tools extensively to decide which positions and issues to emphasize. In the case of the Argentinean PRO, these tools were first used while the party governed the city of Buenos Aires and other small cities in the province of Buenos Aires. The PRO then used the same tools for subsequent electoral campaigns. The incorporation of technology to collect information about citizens' preferences and local-level issues has been especially useful in the context of weakened party organizations (as in Chile) and new organizations (such as the Argentinean PRO).

In parties with denser organizational structures, the incorporation of technology and, in particular, the use of systems to integrate information can complement the territorial work of the party but it also raises concerns about the final use of these tools. In Uruguay in 2017, the FA incorporated a tool to integrate and manage information about its adherents and aggregate information from public sources (e.g. census and electoral results). Even though party authorities expressed enthusiasm about the potential of this tool, party activists questioned its cost and usefulness.

Sartori (1976) states that "parties provide something that no poll or machine can supply: They transmit demands *backed by pressure.*[1] The party throws its own weight into the demands it feels compelled to respond to" (25). As Sartori wisely observed, politics is not the simple aggregation and prioritization of citizens' preferences. Rather, politics implies the complex interaction of preferences, values, and both the institutional and the political context, where citizens

---

[1] Italics in the original.

need agents to act on their behalf. While in a democracy parties cannot be replaced by a tool to collect preferences and an algorithm that aggregates them to produce policies, doing so is plausible within party organizations. As we argued earlier, political parties can collect member preferences in different ways to decide which ones to express, and which issues to prioritize through internal decision-making processes. This decision-making is mediated by the structural traits of the party's internal organization, where different methods of capturing citizens' preferences affect the distribution of power within the party, the preferences prioritized, and the resulting decisions. When members are replaced by tools used to survey citizens' preferences, the politics within the party disappears. In such cases, preferences are not "backed by pressure," and leaders are not constrained by different constituencies represented within the party. In this scenario, members lose their power as persuaders (Downs 1957), that is, as people who know what people want, vis-à-vis party leaders. In these settings, only the preferences of the median voter, or those positions on which the median voter feels indifferent, would be considered as potential party stances. Finally, social organizations also lose their power vis-à-vis parties as a means to inform parties about citizens' preferences (Anria et al. 2022).

Finally, political parties organize and mobilize voters to win elections. They reduce the cost of turnout and of informing voters (Aldrich 1995). As a result, political parties are institutions through which ambitious politicians can pursue political careers. Traditionally, cadre and mass-organic political parties relied on volunteers to organize campaigns in the field and to mobilize voters. The popularization of media such as radio and TV changed the PCO from the Mass PCO to the Broadcast PCO (Epstein 2018). Mass media reduced the need for volunteers to spread candidates' and parties' messages, and thus reduced the need for volunteers to fulfill the function of reducing the cost of information for voters. This engendered organizational transformations that led to the emergence of professional electoral parties (Katz and Mair 1994; Panebianco 1988). The emergence of new technologies and the shift from the Broadcast PCO to the Information PCO engendered new opportunities to mount campaigns in the field (Nielsen 2012).

Before new ICTs became a "mundane tool" (Nielsen 2011), campaign organizing required the incorporation of activists in a group with a territorial reference (e.g. a neighborhood, city, or factory). In the past, when a party organization called on members to engage in party activities, the members were transformed not only into activists but also into party stakeholders. When party sympathizers become stakeholders, they increase their power vis-à-vis leaders, because they acquire the power to keep leaders accountable. Previously, it was impossible to build an army of volunteers without activating them politically within the party by engaging them as a group within the party structure.

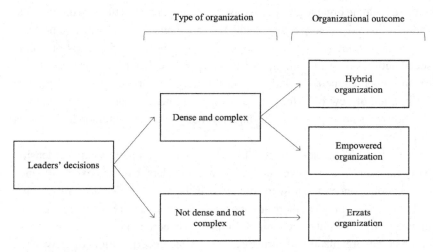

**Figure 2** The incorporation of new ICTs and the organizational outcome.

ICTs. New ICTs as a substitute for party organization provide a cheaper and less time-consuming way of selecting candidates, collecting citizens' preferences, and deploying people in the field to campaign, without having to wait for the long-term returns associated with investing in developing a traditional organizational structure in the territory. In these cases, the incorporation of technology is limited only by leaders' preferences and exogenous factors.

The adoption of new ICTs in this scenario substitutes for the conventional organization in the recruitment of candidates. Thus, the process of recruitment and candidate selection is highly centralized by the leader and the campaign team. In this setting, candidates might be recruited using open online calls. In turn, leaders at the national level identify and select candidates. The recruited candidates do not need to have previous ties to the campaign, to the voters, or to other candidates. New ICTs that are incorporated in the absence of an organization also substitute for the traditional organization function of collecting information about citizens' preferences and demands, especially at the local level. Social listening tools, sometimes in conjunction with administrative data, provide granular information. These tools provide campaigns with the capacity to monitor what occurs in the territory without needing to rely on volunteers who reside in the area. In the past, before these technologies were available, there was no option but to convene the volunteers of one neighborhood or area and, because the campaign lacked detailed information from the territory, it had to transfer responsibility to neighborhood leaders and local campaign managers to decide how to operate locally. Finally, in terms of mobilization, new ICTs allow campaigns to mobilize people without building organic groups. Sympathizers are identified through online calls, and they are individually engaged with the campaign. They are asked to perform individual actions (e.g. to share content via instant messaging apps or online social networks), or they are invited to take part in collective actions that do not require much cooperation and coordination (e.g. to participate in a rally). The substitution of new ICTs for people in the fulfillment of parties' organizational functions engenders parties with a high level of power concentration in the hands of the leaders.

In parties with greater levels of organizational complexity and/or density, party rank-and-file, and eventually grassroots leaders, can also exert influence on decisions concerning how to adopt new ICTs. When leaders face a party that is dense and/or complex, there are two possible outcomes: a hybrid organization that partially substitutes technology for people in certain party functions; or, an empowered organizational structure, where the incorporation of new ICTs boosts the organizational capacity of people in performing party functions.

In the hybrid outcome, the incorporation of new ICTs entails the coexistence of new ICTs with a permanent organization that already fulfills the three functions (recruitment, information, and mobilization). When the adoption partially substitutes for conventional organization, the result is the coexistence of conventional organizational structures with procedures that employ new ICTs' enabled platforms. In most places, candidates are recruited conventionally, through party bodies, but, in others, where the organization is weaker, they might be recruited through open calls or by using new ICTs to screen prospective candidates. The party incorporates social listening tools to inform decisions about which issues to politicize and the positions of the party. Traditional collective bodies of local participation and deliberation coexist with the mobilization of adherents through their individual activation using online platforms and instant messaging apps centrally controlled by the party leadership.

In the empowering outcome, the adoption of new ICTs empowers the rank-and-file when the leadership fails or opts not to substitute organization for technology, and the organization incorporates new ICTs to boost its available capacities. In this scenario, the adoption of new ICTs does not transform candidate recruitment and selection. However, it does change the processes of information collection and adherent mobilization. Social listening and the processing of administrative or publicly available data are employed to inform the organization and improve its deployment in the field, thus empowering the role of organizers. In terms of mobilization, new ICTs are used to incorporate adherents into the organizational structure rather than to simply use them for electoral mobilization purposes in campaign activities defined solely by the leadership.

Grecia Street,[3] completely different; however, you do not have that atomization of messaging from the perspective of the candidate (Antonio Diaz-Araujo, Unholster, Chile).

Parties and campaigns use the geolocation of electoral and other administrative data to build heat maps of prospective voters in the field. This technology allows campaigns to decide where to invest their efforts in the territory and identify the geographic location of likely voters. Giorgio Jackson, from Revolución Democrática (Democratic Revolution, RD) in Chile, described what is offered as follows: "In Chile, you have an analysis of geolocation by socioeconomic level and historical voting results at the level of the polling station ( ... ) They sell you a very basic analysis." (Giorgio Jackson, RD, Chile). The same kind of service is offered in Costa Rica and in Argentina (Rolando Rodríguez, CAMEDIA, Costa Rica; and Luciano Galup, consultant, Argentina).

Parties and campaigns also use new technologies to recruit and manage volunteers. Jorge Selume, an advisor to former Chilean president Sebastián Piñera, mentioned that:

> People register on a platform, on a landing page. It is like a webpage, but simpler and lighter. Generally, one asks people to give their email, and then you ask them questions about the things that interest them ( ... ) you start generating your own databases. These are assets that must be administered over time ( ... ) because tomorrow you want these people go to the polls and vote for you. (Jorge Selume, Artool, Chile).

Guillermo Riera, the person in charge of digital political communication for the PRO in the 2015 presidential election in Argentina, said that the PRO developed a web application where adherents could register to become campaign volunteers. The same strategy was pursued in the presidential campaign of Rodolfo Hernández in Colombia in 2022. People joined the campaign and provided contacts that were organized in a network using the software Wappid (Juan Manuel Corredor, Wappid and advisor to Rodolfo Hernández for the 2022 Colombia presidential campaign). Landing pages are sometimes also used to recruit prospective local leaders. This was used, for example, by the PRO in Argentina, by the Rodolfo Hernández campaign in Colombia, and by Evópoli in Chile. The following excerpt from an interview with the national territorial coordinator of Evópoli illustrates this use:

> we created a platform called «community leaders» in which we invited independents to join a campaign to become a candidate for local councils. For us, these elections are the most important because it is a way of building a long-term

---

[3] Villa Frei is a lower-middle-class neighborhood located in an otherwise relatively wealthy commune.

organic structure at the local level. So, we invited people to be part of this project, and people signed up. They had tests, they had hurdles, and we conducted an assessment because we did not want just to track the evolution of numbers, but, rather, to know whom we are incorporating, and to learn each person's story ( . . .) The entire process was automated on a platform, with figures, filters, where each region had a person in charge of this process, and each region had someone who was monitoring what each of the registered prospective candidates was doing (Felipe O'Ryan, Evópoli, Chile).

Instant messaging apps facilitate the organization of volunteers and make it possible to disseminate messages without the need for intermediaries. This technology is increasingly used as an internal channel of communication for campaign organizers and to mobilize broader communities of supporters (Treré 2020). Luciano Galup mentioned that his firm has developed: "a map of localities from which we generate polygons, that are composed of three or four blocks, each has a digital referent that has to build a digital community [of candidates' supporters] in WhatsApp in that territory" (Luciano Galup, consultant, Argentina). Instant messaging apps are also used to disseminate campaign messages and propaganda employing communities of supporters to amplify such messages among their personal contacts. Several campaigns, such as those of Bolsonaro in Brazil, have also used the end-to-end encrypted nature of these apps (i.e. their lack of editorial control) to promote the viral spreading of misinformation and fake news (Bastos dos Santos et al. 2019; Davis and Straubhaar 2020; Evangelista and Bruno 2019; Piaia and Alves 2020; Resende et al. 2019). Different parties (e.g. the PRO in Argentina or the FA in Uruguay) have used WhatsApp or other instant messaging apps to coordinate campaign actions on social networks to amplify the conversation around specific issues or candidates.

There is a diffusion and transfer of knowledge between parties of the same ideological family in the region. In terms of diffusion, Juan José López Murphy, from the firm Globant in Uruguay, mentioned that:

[These technologies] spread easily between parties. If something was used in Brazil, in Argentina, or it was used in Chile, other countries in the region are going to adopt it. Political consultants tend to migrate. They export the modus operandi. When something has been effective, it spreads very quickly (Juan José López Murphy, Globant, Uruguay).

In terms of transfer of knowledge, in the case of Uruguay, according to members of Daniel Martínez's campaign team (presidential candidate of the FA in the 2019 presidential election), the leftist Brazilian Partido dos Trabalhadores (Workers' Party, PT) advised and trained his campaign personnel. In the final stretch of the presidential campaign, there were PT members working in

Uruguay on big data and segmentation for the FA campaign (anonymous member of the Broad Front campaign team, Uruguay). There has also been transfer of know-how in other cases, such as from the center-right Argentinean PRO to the presidential campaign of center-right politician Sebastián Piñera in Chile in 2017 (Federico Morales, PRO, Argentina).

## Data Availability: Party Databases, Public Records, and Commercial Databases

In Latin America, there generally is a scarcity of public data available for electoral campaigns. Furthermore, parties and campaigns lack the material resources or the organizational capacity to generate them, either from social networks or from field organizing work. These conditions, as well as the lack of financial resources, limit what parties and campaigns can do with new ICTs. Mauro Granese, from Evópoli, mentioned that:

> In terms of variables, it is very basic [what we can use]; sociodemographic variables, age, preferences, tastes, etc. Sometimes this is used together with other publicly available data, but it is a basic analysis. In the US they integrate much more information, they use credit card data. In Chile, you cannot do that ( ... ) In the US they spend a billion dollars, it is crazy what they can do (Mauro Granese, Evópoli, Chile).

Regarding the type of data that parties have about their supporters and the data that parties can generate, Rolando Rodríguez from CAMEDIA summarizes the situation in Costa Rica, which is similar to the situation described by different service providers for other countries:

> They are very simple databases. They have databases, but they are very messy. They are not integrated ( ... ) There are some parties that have been more systematic in the use of technology. There are parties that have their webpages and social networks, and with that, they obtain some data. However, the traffic generated by these webpages is very low (Rolando Rodríguez, CAMEDIA, Costa Rica).

Parties with greater organizational capacity have more and better information about their adherents, accumulated and structured over several electoral campaigns. However, even in these cases the quality is not optimal to take full advantage of new ICTs. This occurs because of the lack of investment in updating and curating those databases. For example, Francisco Chacón from the PLN mentioned that:

> We have extensive databases. We have had data from our open party conventions for many years now; we have registered the data of participants. [We have] a database of about 500,000 people. It was used to send SMS and

WhatsApp messages, not with the intensity that we would have wished because it is not a refined and updated database (Francisco Chacón, PLN, Costa Rica).

The Unión Demócrata Independiente (Democratic Independent Union, UDI) another established Chilean party with a well-developed organization, shows that these databases are party assets that are available for party candidates at different levels:

> the database of adherents is available even to party activists ( ... ) parallel to that, each authority or each person who performs territorial work has his or her own database, in that sense the party's database is common ground. For example, five candidates for the municipal council from the same municipality have the same database of adherents, this is the foundation for them, and they later build their own parallel or joint databases (Camila Gonzales, UDI, Chile).

There are publicly available administrative data, essentially census and electoral data. Besides the data analytics derived from social listening in social networks, electoral and census data are the basic sources for the analysis offered by the firms to parties and campaigns. Interviewees, both new ICT service providers and politicians, acknowledge that there are firms that offer commercial databases, such as mobile phone companies, credit records, and credit card records, among others. Other firms sell audiences with defined profiles for advertising on social networks, such as football team fans. However, none of our interviewees (neither providers nor politicians) acknowledged offering, buying, or using these kinds of databases, though interviewees claim that these commercial databases can be used – and are used – due to a lack of enforcement of data privacy rules. Gabriel Camargo from the firm Ingenious in Uruguay said:

> Here, it does happen ( ... ) In Uruguay, if you need a database, that database appears. In Argentina and Brazil, it is worse. A campaign manager who does not want to lose is going to press all the necessary buttons. The firm has to decide whether to use data that it perhaps should not have at all ( ... ) There is regulation, and in Uruguay the data privacy regulation is appropriate, but it is a dead letter (Gabriel Camargo, Ingenious, Uruguay).

Andrés Couble, from RD in Chile, expressed the same view: "In Chile, [personal data protection] regulation is very outdated and apart from that it is weakly enforced" (Andrés Couble, RD, Chile).

## How Service Providers and Politicians Assess the Incorporation of New ICTs

The actual incorporation of new ICTs requires various services and the development of products but, as in any other market, consumers need to know the potential benefits of such products and services and how to use them, that is, successful new ICT incorporation requires technological readiness (Parasuraman 2000). Diego Piñeiro synthesizes what we have been told in different in-depth interviews regarding the technological readiness of parties and candidates: "The demand is still in its infancy. We have had to preach a lot to develop projects" (Diego Piñeiro, Ideia, Uruguay). In general, Latin American parties and candidates are curious about new ICTs and how they might be used. At the same time, however, there is a degree of distrust regarding the potential benefits of these tools. Therefore, parties and candidates are somewhat reluctant to allocate financial resources to these tools and they perceive the opportunity cost associated with new ICTs as high, given the other campaign uses to which limited funds could be put. Pablo Buela, from the Uruguayan firm PIMOD, illustrates this issue as follows: "I have worked for the traditional parties [in Uruguay]. [They are] very interested in the new [ICTs], but when it comes to budget decisions, [they] keep making decisions like before" (Pablo Buela, PIMOD, Uruguay).

The lack of knowledge about the main features of the new ICTs and their potential for electoral purposes parallels politicians' misperceptions regarding the costs of adopting these technologies and their efficacy. As Gabriel Camargo, from the Uruguayan firm Ingenious, notes: "There is a perception that this is very expensive, and it is true, but people think it is more expensive than it actually is" (Gabriel Camargo, Ingenious, Uruguay). Notwithstanding politicians' perceptions about the cost of incorporating new ICTs, the actual costs involve more than simply buying ads on social networks and on other digital platforms. In Gabriel Camargo's account (as for other providers), using new ICTs also involves developing tools, digital platforms, and hiring a team of experts. Thus, this entails redirecting resources that were previously allocated to traditional campaign items.

As mentioned before, Latin American political campaigns do not have access to the financial resources available in the US setting. Thus, the capacity to employ new ICTs to their fullest potential is essentially limited to high-profile campaigns. Jorge Selume, a Chilean consultant who worked for the presidential campaign of Sebastián Piñera in 2017 and for other campaigns for the Chilean Right, emphasizes that congressional campaigns are amateurs in terms of the use of new ICTs and therefore they are not an "attractive market" for providers. Only presidential campaigns can afford professional teams (Jorge Selume, consultant, Chile). Moreover, Sebastián Krajlevich, a Chilean political consultant, mentioned that well-resourced campaigns rely on different service providers for different tasks coordinated by the campaign general manager.[4]

---

[4] In Chile, firms work with only one side of the ideological spectrum, while in Uruguay firms tend to work with all the parties or candidates in different elections or even in the same election (Diego Barcia, Nicestream and Illuminati, Uruguay and Sebastián Krajlevich, consultant, Chile).

Regardless of the financial costs of using new ICTs during electoral campaigns, politicians also highlighted that having a permanent in-house data team is unaffordable for most parties:

> This is normally outsourced, firstly because it is very expensive to maintain a professional team that you create in-house from scratch. Our party is new and does not have the [public] funding for that level of internal development. There are companies that are dedicated to this and they have lowered the prices a lot. It is easy to bring in their expertise and it is quicker to implement it than to start [to develop these capacities in-house] from scratch (Francisco Prendas, Nueva República, Costa Rica).

In general, political parties in Latin America have weak organizational structures and lack the capacity to develop their own ICT infrastructure; nor are they able to plan ahead and invest in ICT development before the electoral campaigns. As a result, decisions to incorporate new ICTs typically are made by electoral campaigns when they are already on the campaign trail (Gonzalo Roqué, Roque Marketing Insights, Argentina; Guillermo Spinelli, Quanam, Uruguay; and José Chacín, Partido por la Democracia (Party for Democracy, PPD), Chile; among others). Rolando Rodríguez from the firm CAMEDIA in Costa Rica mentioned that, "The structures of the political parties are so weak that [data intelligence structures] cannot be maintained during non-electoral years" (Rolando Rodríguez, CAMEDIA, Costa Rica). Similarly, Roberto Gallardo from the PLN in Costa Rica said that "the activity of political parties in [the] country decreases between elections" (Roberto Gallardo, PLN, Costa Rica).

Parties rely on the knowledge or expertise of some members or activists to make the decisions regarding the incorporation of new ICTs and to interact with providers in the daily campaign operations. These people are usually volunteers. The following excerpts from our in-depth interviews with politicians illustrate that this seems to be the norm across different cases:

> for electoral intelligence work there is a very rudimentary analysis that we do internally, with very basic technology, with tools for database analysis ( . . . ) In terms of technology for electoral campaigns, everything has been outsourced ( . . . ) we do not have the capacity within the party. (Giorgio Jackson, RD, Chile).

> [during campaigns] external companies are hired to do social network analytics ( . . . ) The in-house capacities are basic. They are people with an almost self-taught, basic level of knowledge. In practice, the type of professional who has these professional skills has salaries that are beyond what the party can afford (Anthony Cascante, PAC, Costa Rica).

The party is somewhat behind in terms of managing the database. However, there are members within the party who are experts in this area. So, usually, during the elections, these members come to help, but it is not a permanent [contribution]. For this reason, we are lagging. This task is only performed during elections (José Chacín, PPD, Chile).

Alberto Espinoza from the Chilean firm Dinámica Pública emphasized that this lack of professionalism within parties limits their ability to use new ICTs and data to their fullest potential, both during campaigns and between electoral periods. Parties prefer to receive reports from the providers rather than building capacity within the organization to develop their own data and reports; they prefer pdf files rather than dashboards.

Political parties in Latin America are at an incipient stage in terms of developing in-house expertise and incorporating new ICTs for their daily operations. Parties use standard software to organize their members (e.g. Google Apps or Microsoft Office) because of their relative simplicity and ease of use: "If we can do it with Google apps, we do it with Google apps, because you save money, you save time, you do not have to explain to anyone how to use it. In fact, we do some online surveys, and we use Google Forms, we do not invent anything" (Luciano Galup, consultant, Argentina). Similarly, Gonzalo Díaz of RD in Chile said:

> RD usually does not have a lot of financial resources, and the teams are usually volunteers and people who are not experts in what I would call big data technologies. So, the technologies used are mostly Google Forms, Google Sheets (Gonzalo Díaz, RD, Chile).

There is also a problem of technological readiness at the local level to incorporate technology and data management in field operations. It seems not to be enough for people in the field to have access to technological tools, like smartphones with internet connection and instant messaging apps; they also need to have the disposition and competence to incorporate new ICTs, especially specific software. The following excerpt from an in-depth interview with a right-wing party bureaucrat in Chile illustrates this:

> [The] general secretary of the party [at the time] put me in contact with a firm that was offering a very interesting service for mayoral candidates. They had mapped each municipality entirely with a territorial viewer. [In this viewer] you could click on each house, and you could mark [the house] with the colors of a traffic light: green if there are people who are going to vote for you and you would go visit them later; yellow, if you have to convince them; and red, those houses to which you should not return. The funny thing is that it had different users so each brigade member could have the application and mark. We bought the demo from this firm, we applied it in three municipalities, one

from Santiago, one from a large region and one from [another] region ( . . . ) It was a disaster in all three and our conclusion was that it was a disaster because the brigade members [did not incorporate it in the field]. They all had smartphones, they all had WhatsApp, etc., but they forgot to turn it on, they forgot to use it, there is no culture of using technology (anonymous, right-wing party bureaucrat, Chile).[5]

Despite this general picture, some parties incorporate software to perform organizational tasks. For example, the Partido Unidad Social Cristiana (Social Christian Unity Party, PUSC) developed a Sistema de Inscripción y Registro de Información Electoral en Línea (Online Electoral Information and Registration System, SIRIEL). It cost the party USD 70,000 and it facilitates not only voter registration for internal elections but also the administration of the party member database. The system allows the PUSC to communicate by text message with those who sign up in the system (Anabelle Lang, PUSC, Costa Rica). The Uruguayan FA bought a software package called "Quilt" to manage and integrate data of adherents with data from administrative records (e.g. electoral and census data). The PRO in Argentina developed its own software to manage volunteers during electoral campaigns. A small party in Costa Rica, Vamos (Let's Go) uses the platform NationBuilder to manage its adherents.

The incorporation of technology is not only limited by the availability of resources and organizational capacities but also by the levels of internal fragmentation and the tensions between the central authority and the local leaders. Parties in Latin America are organizationally weak and are also fragmented in their daily operations. Although in national elections there might be a nationwide campaign managed by the party's national leaders, there are also multiple campaigns around different candidates at different levels (national, regional, and local). In this scenario, parties are unable to centralize the strategy to collect, manage, and use data for two main reasons. First, candidates at the district level do not have the financial resources to incorporate new ICTs. Excessive fragmentation in a context of lack of resources precludes costly investments in organizational developments that entail economies of scale. Second, when central authorities are weak and do not accumulate and concentrate organizational capacities, data management is scattered and unstructured. This is an important issue even in a centralized and unitary country such as Chile: "there are no digital teams in charge of centralizing and implementing strategies to manage databases. So, the person in charge of Punta Arenas has his database and manages it, the person in charge of Arica has his [own database]" (Enzo Abbagliati, Factor Crítico, Chile). Providers, in turn, respond to this

---

[5] This interviewee requested anonymity.

fragmentation by negotiating with individual candidates (Giorgio Jackson, RD, Chile). Also, in the Argentinean Partido Justicialista (Justicialist Party, PJ) there is no centralized management of a database of adherents and activists. What does exist are databases that were developed in a decentralized manner at the level of mayors and governors, though not homogeneously developed throughout the country. The lack of party organization limits party leaders' incentives of to centrally invest in data infrastructure. Yet some factions with territorial penetration, such as La Cámpora, succeeded in creating a national database (anonymous advisor to Alberto Fernández's 2019 campaign, Argentina). Marcos Salazar, an advisor to the PLN in Costa Rica stated:

> No, it does not exist [a relationship between the territorial work and new ICTs]. Because, to begin with, the PLN has territorial fiefdoms, and it is difficult to have a single national territorial strategy. There is a general line, but everyone has their way. The PLN leaders [at the local level] are not people who use technology. They have Excel databases or things like that. There is not a unified data strategy, everyone has their little notebook (Marco Salazar, Advisor, Costa Rica).

At the local level, there is also an aversion to incorporating new tools. Local leaders believe that they have an extensive knowledge of the field and their potential electorate. Therefore, they perceive these new tools as an unnecessary burden and sometimes view them as a tool central authorities use to control them and challenge their territorial power.

> The teams of the candidates, the teams of the congress members, the mayors, and those who are in the field are very, very precarious and very averse to change. ( . . . ) The problem is that [candidates] do not find it useful ( . . . ) In [the name of his political party in Chile], and in Chile [in general], there is a prevalent belief [among local leaders] that they know their streets, their neighborhoods ( . . . ) and they do not need a compass. Unfortunately, there is a lot of arrogance from territorial leaders (anonymous right-wing politician in Chile).

In this section, we have provided an overview of the services and technologies available to political parties and campaigns in Latin America. Parties and campaigns increasingly have been incorporating new ICTs, especially for electoral campaigns. In almost all cases that we have surveyed, parties and campaigns buy these services from private firms. The most widely bought service is the analysis that results from social listening in social networks and the segmentation of campaign messages. Even though new ICTs have become increasingly affordable, the financial resources on hand for campaigns and the scarce availability of data limit the use of these technologies.

Besides this general picture, there exists a great degree of variation in the incorporation of new ICTs in the region. Whereas presidential campaigns have the resources to buy technological services and hire teams of experts, this is not the case for congressional and, especially, for local elections. In these lower levels, due to the scarcity of financial and human resources, new ICTs are incorporated to a lesser degree and their use is less professional. In established parties with dense organizational structures, the lack of technological readiness of local leaders and their general aversion to changing traditional practices also limits the effective deployment of new ICTs.

## The Cases

In this section, we describe five cases of incorporation of new ICTs in different types of electoral vehicles in Latin America. From weakly organized independents to institutionalized parties, we survey how various new technologies have been incorporated to fulfill some or all of the functions that parties fulfill for electoral mobilization and organization. These are heuristic case studies (George and Bennett 2005) and provide descriptive inferences of the process of incorporation of new ICTs. We have conducted fieldwork in Argentina (PRO), Chile (LdP), Colombia (Rodolfo Hernández), and Uruguay (PN and FA). The evidence comes from in-depth interviews with party leaders, activists, and consultants who have worked in campaigns for these electoral vehicles.

The cases of Rodolfo Hernández in Colombia and the LdP in Chile illustrate the incorporation of new ICTs to forge an ersatz organization. Both processes of incorporation show how substituting new ICTs for people and organizational structure limits a party's ability to engender permanent and complex collective action. The case of the PRO in Argentina illustrates a case where the incorporation of new ICTs to perform some of the party functions previously carried out by people leads to a hybrid organization, where individual engagement coexists with traditional forms of engagement with the organization (collective engagement). Finally, the cases of the FA and the PN in Uruguay illustrate how the adoption of new ICTs can face challenges, especially when the incorporation of new ICTs does not confer a clear benefit for grassroots activists or for faction and local leaders.

## Rodolfo Hernández & the LIGA

New ICTs have reduced the costs of electoral campaigning and, in turn, have made it easier for outsiders to enter the political arena. These outsiders or independent candidates, who lack an organizational structure, do not face organizational constraints on incorporating new ICTs. They do not face party stakeholders who might block the decision or dilute it. In weakly organized or nonexistent structures, the adoption of new ICTs is thus determined only by exogenous factors and leaders' willingness. Nonetheless, the reduction of the costs to contact people and engage them in campaigns does not eliminate the need to have organizers to manage supporters. The incorporation of new ICTs is restricted by the capacity and/or the decision of leaders to invest in personnel to organize supporters. Contacting and connecting supporters through instant messaging apps does not automatically engender a community with the capacity to carry out political actions aligned with the campaign's goals. Campaigns still depend on organizers to lead or to identify prospective leaders within groups of supporters. This is crucial to assign responsibilities and tasks to develop complex collective action. Without the division of labor engendered by organizers, groups of supporters lack the capacity to coordinate between different necessary roles to collectively commit to perform complex campaign activities in a harmonized fashion. In this scenario, technology engenders an ersatz organization that lacks the ability to perform complex organizational tasks.

Some authors have claimed that new ICTs bolstered the capacity of people to engage in political action through less hierarchical and decentralized networks (Bimber, Flanagin, and Stohl 2012; Vaccari and Valeriani 2016). These networks enable people to produce and distribute propaganda on an individual basis. Nonetheless, in these instances collective action is limited to actions that do not require much division of labor. The incorporation of new ICTs still needs organizers to engender strategic, ongoing collective action. Thus, the candidates' decision and capacity to invest in developing a structure of organizers, or to rely on already available mobilizational structures (c.f. Van Dyck 2021), still determines the potential for expanding people's collective action capacity in campaigns and the limits of technology to empower people in politics.

The presidential campaign of Rodolfo Hernández in Colombia in 2022 illustrates how an independent candidate was able to successfully contact and mobilize many supporters. Hernández's campaign did not have any structured organization and had no access to available mobilizational structures. It relied on a handful of inexperienced staff. Hernández took advantage of the affordability of new ICTs to reach prospective supporters and build WhatsApp groups across Colombia. Even though Hernández's campaign was successful in reaching thousands of prospective supporters across the country, it was unable to organize supporters in the field to perform intense canvassing, coordinated mobilization for the election day, and poll watching.

The campaign contacted 561,000 people using Wappid and connected them in 2,870 WhatsApp groups across the country. The Wappid software develops a network of supporters based on referrals in a manner that resembles network marketing structures. Supporters within the network gain prominence by increasing the membership of the network.

In 2022, Rodolfo Hernández ran as an independent presidential candidate, after collecting more than a million signatures, under the personalistic label the LIGA. He campaigned with an antipolitics stance and emphasized the fight against corruption as his main campaign motto. Hernández's personalistic movement was devoid of an organizational structure, had minimal material and human resources, and relied on a handful of volunteers and advisors who lacked expertise in electoral politics. He ran an austere, self-funded campaign and nonetheless obtained an unexpectedly successful electoral result in the first round of the presidential campaign. With almost six million votes, 28.2 percent of the total, Hernández came in second and competed in the runoff. In the second round he received 47.3 percent of the votes, losing to Gustavo Petro.[6]

Hernández's intensive use of new ICTs to communicate, especially through social networks like Facebook, date back to his mayoral campaign in 2015. The low-cost use of Facebook, mainly based on organic use, aligned with his austere approach to campaigning. The organic growth of his messages in social networks allowed him to reach a broad audience and to attract followers. He portrayed himself as a political outsider who fights against the political establishment and its corrupt practices using new means of communication. His presidential campaign in 2022 followed the same austerity pattern. He decided to self-fund his presidential bid. He did not accept private contributions nor the public electoral subsidy.[7]

Since 2020, Hernández used Facebook to address his followers weekly via live streaming. During these events he discussed political issues. Facebook groups of followers were organically created with some volunteers acting as administrators. By the end of 2021, one such volunteer, Andrés Cabrera, a fervent supporter of Hernández, began using WhatsApp to group supporters in different cities across Colombia. When Hernández began his presidential bid, Cabrera was put in charge of the campaign volunteers. Soon after, Cabrera contacted Juan Manuel Corredor, the developer of Wappid. Hernández decided to hire Corredor and to use his software to build communities of supporters. This software was seen as an opportunity to rapidly build a network of supporters for a campaign that lacked any organizational structure.

---

[6] Gustavo Petro is a leftist politician who was the presidential candidate of the Pacto Histórico (Historical Pact) coalition in the 2022 presidential coalition.

[7] Hernández spent approximately USD 1.2 million while his main rival, Gustavo Petro, spent around USD 7.3 million. Source: Cuentas Claras. www.cnecuentasclaras.gov.co/ (last accessed May 24, 2023) and "¿Cuánto gastaron todas las campañas presidenciales en Colombia?" (*Portafolio*, July 17, 2022). www.portafolio.co/economia/finanzas/cuanto-gastaron-todas-las-campanas-presidenciales-en-colombia-568281 (last accessed May 24, 2023).

Hernández's network of supporters grew exponentially. Hernández's campaign WhatsApp groups helped to mount his campaign all over Colombia. The calls to join caravans and other campaign meetings were spread through the groups. In these groups, Hernández supporters shared messages in favor of the candidate and against opponents. Stickers, memes, and slogans designed by users were shared and forwarded, people were invited to vote on Election Day, and some users offered their vehicles to transport people to the polls. All the activity in the groups was spontaneously performed, without a strategic plan or resources.

Hernández's decision to run an austere campaign and the lack of any organizational support severely limited his capacity to organize people in the field. Hernández's campaign staff comprised a handful of advisors and only ten organizers (Ana León and Anderson Villalba Rey, La Silla Vacía, Colombia). The few organizers hired by the campaign could not manage the numerous WhatsApp groups and lacked the tools needed to carry out their duties effectively. This lack of organizers limited the effective use of the network of supporters for electoral purposes.

There were few posts in the Hernández supporters' WhatsApp groups about the organization of campaign activities. Most of the content posted to the WhatsApp groups concerned the ideological position of Hernández, religious references, and anti-Petro stances. The content shared in the groups was not material produced by the campaign. One-third of the posts in the groups that we followed were multimedia files (4,737 out of 15,285) and 1,701 were links to other platforms (YouTube and Facebook). These features characterize campaign WhatsApp groups in other campaigns in Latin America (see e.g. Machado et al. 2019).

In the WhatsApp groups that we followed it was not possible to identify any division of labor. Groups' administrators did not play a significant role. They did not perform organizational tasks (online or offline), distribute official campaign content, or lead or moderate the conversation within the groups. Administrators were not the most active users (those who posted more messages). In our sample, administrators were not among the twenty-five most active users. In an in-depth interview, Andrés Cabrera emphasized that the lack of community managers to work with the WhatsApp groups limited the campaign interaction with them. The campaign was not able to support and guide the supporters (Andrés Cabrera, manager of Hernández's campaign volunteers, Colombia).

The few offline campaign activities featured low organizational complexity and did not entail the allocation of significant campaign resources. For example, caravans were a common activity in the Hernández campaign. According to

Andrés Cabrera, Hernández did not invest a single peso in these events. The advertising that accompanied the caravans, t-shirts, hats, and stickers with various logos, slogans, and color combinations were designed and produced by volunteers who did not receive any compensation (Andrés Cabrera, manager of Hernández's campaign volunteers, Colombia).

The use of new ICTs was also not accompanied by a parallel investment in organizers dedicated to coordinating activities and developing campaign tasks that entail complex collective action. The campaign was successful in engaging people using Wappid, and in grouping these people in WhatsApp groups at the city or municipal level. Nonetheless, the campaign could not exploit the data collected to distribute personalized messages or assign personalized tasks (Ana León, La Silla Vacía, Colombia). Juan Manuel Corredor, the creator and CEO of Wappid and Hernández campaign advisor, also emphasized in an in-depth interview that the campaign's difficulty exploiting data was attributable to the scarcity of financial resources: "collecting the data is tough, but administering it is even tougher and more costly" (Juan Manuel Corredor, Wappid, Colombia).

The lack of investment in organizers and in developing an organizational structure negatively affected the returns of Wappid. The candidate paid no attention to the platform and did not consider it necessary to coordinate the campaign team or to organize supporters in the field. This is observed in the absence of a strategic development of the field operation and the role of volunteers. There were no attempts to develop get-out-the-vote campaigns in each district. Volunteers were eager to act; for example some offered transportation to take voters to the polls. However, the campaign neither deployed any coordinated action nor encouraged volunteers to take action on Election Day. Messages posted by volunteers like the following appeared in the WhatsApp groups: "On Election Day, those of us who have a car, make it available to those people who don't have transportation to their polling station" (WhatsApp Group in Manizales).

The same pattern was observed in the absence of a strategy to recruit and deploy people to serve as poll watchers on Election Day. Supporters in the WhatsApp groups (not administrators) called members to become poll watchers (Corredor 2022). In the different WhatsApp groups, supporters indicated how to become a poll watcher. In the days before the election, people asked in the WhatsApp groups for information about the status of their registration as poll watchers, but they did not receive any answer. On the day before the runoff, a user posted this message in one of Cali's WhatsApp groups: "Attention campaign administrators: please, we have had no positive answer about our badges to serve as poll watchers, we need an answer, please." Those who showed up as poll watchers also did not receive any logistical support from the campaign throughout the day. As León stated: "to deploy poll watchers requires an infrastructure, a logistics that requires a minimum amount of money that Rodolfo did not provide" (Ana León, La Silla Vacía, Colombia).

The Hernández campaign was able to attract and connect thousands of supporters by taking advantage of new ICTs, especially through instant messaging apps. However, the case also illustrates the limits of this strategy if one cannot rely on an existing organizational structure and does not hire organizers who can administer the people in the field. This case highlights the importance of distinguishing between the capacity to contact prospective supporters and even to mobilize them in an unorganized fashion and campaigns that employ new ICTs in combination with a structure that is able to organize supporters in the field. Whereas in the latter new ICTs boost organizational capacities, in the former new ICTs enable the building an ersatz organization.

## Lista del Pueblo

New ICTs bolster the capacity of people to coordinate a common national brand among prospective candidates in different districts. In the absence of an available nationwide organization, new ICTs help to connect prospective candidates at the district level with national entrepreneurs who promote a new electoral brand. Candidates are contacted using different tools and even through open online calls. These candidates do not need to have any previous ties to other candidates at the district or the national level. In a context of discontent with established parties, new ICTs also bolster the capacity of a new brand to rapidly become focal for electoral coordination (Cox 1997). As a result, as Bimber, Flanagin, and Stohl (2012) claim, new ICTs help to rapidly build a nonhierarchical and decentralized network around the new brand. Successful electoral coordination, however, does not necessarily give rise to successful horizontal coordination while in office. Chile's Lista del Pueblo (The People's List, LdP) in the election of constitutional assembly members in 2021 is a case in point.

In October 2019, a wave of massive protests erupted in Chile. The intense mobilization was accompanied by violence, repression, and institutional instability. Until the COVID-19 pandemic hit Chile in March 2020, the country lived under a state of siege and witnessed scenes of violent police repression and massive social mobilizations. In these protests, there was no nationwide organization leading the protests. On November 15, 2019 most political parties in Congress signed the Acuerdo por la Paz y la Nueva Constitución (Agreement for Peace and a New Constitution). This agreement set forth a process to reform the Constitution with the expectation that it would channel discontent through an institutional process and would bring peace to the country. Voters elected constitutional assembly members in a national election on May 15 and 16, 2021.

To legitimize the election of the constitutional assembly members, the Congress passed a bill that partially reformed the constitution to allow groups of independent candidates to run at the district level without the need to fulfill the requirements to become a political party.[8] Before this amendment, independent candidates had to run as individuals. It was almost impossible for independent candidates to compete against party lists that pool votes among several party candidates. Chile has district magnitudes that span from three to eight. To be elected, an independent candidate must obtain more votes than the sum of the votes of all the candidates on a party (or electoral pact) list.[9] The reform reduced the costs of electoral coordination and increased independents' chances of electoral success. To present a list of independents, candidates had to have citizen sponsors equivalent to 0.5 percent of the votes cast in the previous election of representatives in the district, or a minimum of 500 citizens in districts where 0.5 percent of the total number of votes cast in the previous election of representatives was fewer than 500.

Three main groups of lists of independents emerged for the election of constitutional assembly members: LdP, Independientes No Neutrales (Non-Neutral Independents, INN), and Movimientos Sociales Constituyentes (Constitutional Social Movements, MSC). In the election for constitutional assembly members, these lists received 47 out of 155 seats (including the 17 seats reserved for indigenous peoples). The LdP was the most successful list of independents. It presented lists of candidates in 21 out of the 28 electoral districts and it elected 24 out of 138 constitutional assembly members in 20 of the 21 districts where the LdP presented candidates. Even though the LdP spent less than 1/15th as much money as the Lista del Apruebo (List of the

---

[8] Law 21.216 and 21.296 modified the Constitution to allow the formation of electoral lists of independents. The Law also introduced other major unprecedented changes, such as a mechanism to guarantee gender parity in lists of candidates and in the distribution of seats. The Law is publicly available at: www.bcn.cl/leychile/navegar?idNorma=1143661 (last accessed May 25, 2022). To form a political party, an organization must initially comprise at least 100 citizens who do not belong to another political party. Then, the party must register affiliates in all regions where the party will be formally established and the number of affiliates must equal at least 0.25% of the number of voters in the region in the most recent legislative election, or a minimum of 500 voters. A party is constituted after it has been formally organized in eight regions or in at least three contiguous regions.

[9] Parties are allowed to present up to M+1 candidates in their lists on each district. Chile has an open list system. Votes are cast for individual candidates and pooled by list to determine the number of seats allotted to the list.

Approval) that convened the former Concertación parties, it achieved a similar electoral performance.[10]

The LdP was an initiative of a group called El Klan Kiltro (Daniel Trujillo, LdP, Chile). The Klan Kiltro were four social protestors who first met in the streets of downtown Santiago during the protests. They opposed the Acuerdo por la Paz y la Nueva Constitución of November 2019 and decided to build a political platform. The LdP was able to group candidates thanks to the coordination provided by national entrepreneurs who made intensive use of new ICTs. These entrepreneurs reached out to some grassroots leaders and provided an online platform to attract other interested individuals (Rodrigo Urzúa, Carolina Lasalle, and Josefa Faúndez, LdP, Chile). They were able to contact individuals throughout the country who wanted to run as candidates and provided them digital campaign materials with the brand logo. The LdP was able to coordinate and present lists of independent candidates in twenty-one out of the twenty-eight electoral districts without any previous national organization or platform available. This allowed it to pool the free TV broadcast time assigned to each independent candidate and to have a media presence similar to the established parties and electoral pacts.

The lists of the LdP at the district level were essentially local-level initiatives that convened candidates without previous ties to one another (38.1 percent). Before the electoral campaign, only 19.0 percent of the lists of LdP candidates coordinated social or political actions. The different lists of the LdP used various mechanisms of candidate recruitment and selection, though online recruitment was the most frequent (33 percent). The campaign took place during the height of the COVID-19 pandemic. As a result, these lists relied on instant messaging apps and Zoom meetings to coordinate among candidates under a national brand. The LdP, in contrast to the other cases reviewed in this Element, had no software or app designed for electoral purposes or tailored for the LdP.

The candidates of the LdP had connections with different social organizations and movements, especially local or regional organizations. In some cases, these organizations endorsed candidates. Most of these organizations can be defined as either platforms (32.7 percent), that is, networks built around issues that essentially operate on and mobilize using online platforms, such as Fuerza Cultural (Cultural Power), Red Atacameña de Mujeres (Atacameña Network of Women); or civil society groups (30.3 percent) that are formed on the basis of a common nonpolitical social interest, such as social and sports clubs.

---

[10] See "Elección constituyente: las campañas millonarias que fueron derrotadas por candidaturas casi sin fondos" (CIPER, May 17, 2021). www.ciperchile.cl/2021/05/17/eleccion-constitu yente-las-campanas-millonarias-que-fueron-derrotadas-por-candidaturas-casi-sin-fondos/ (last accessed August 27, 2021).

The LdP's success at coordinating among prospective candidates to present lists of candidates throughout the country around a national brand contrasts with its inability to coordinate during the Constitutional Convention (Larrain, Negretto, and Voigt 2023). At the Constitutional Convention, the LdP assembly members had tensions and were not disciplined. Some of its members faced accusations of wrongdoing,[11] and the LdP gradually disintegrated as a caucus.[12] As in the case of Rodolfo Hernández in Colombia, the LdP had no previous organizational structure and, with the help of new ICTs, was able to convene a set of candidates throughout the country. The LdP was a group of candidates from different districts who were recruited by the convenors of the LdP, the Klan Kiltro, using new ICTs. However, as in the case of Hernández, new ICTs produced an ersatz organization. In this case, new ICTs facilitated electoral coordination, though this did not entail the development of organizational capacities to perform political coordination once in office. Both cases show that new ICTs cannot completely substitute for the role people play in traditional organizational structures.

## PRO

New ICTs have enabled political campaigns to contact a massive number of prospective supporters in a personalized way. This affords an opportunity to increase electoral mobilization. However, parties that use new ICTs to increase supporters' engagement with a campaign use it in dissimilar ways (Römmele 2003). In the past, engaging voters with campaigns necessarily entailed incorporating them in a group. New ICTs have eliminated the need for collective instances to gather people to work for the party's candidates. New ICTs have reduced the cost of contacting and organizing prospective campaign volunteers and they enable campaigns to individually engage supporters without making them stakeholders of the organization.

New ICTs facilitate the construction or consolidation of organizational arrangements that can activate people for political action in dissimilar ways. It is crucial to identify how the use of new ICTs promotes different forms of

---

[11] "Condenado por estafa Rodrigo Rojas Vade, el exconstituyente chileno que inventó padecer cáncer," (*El País*, February 13, 2023). https://elpais.com/chile/2023-02-13/condenado-por-estafa-rodrigo-rojas-vade-el-exconstituyente-chileno-que-invento-padecer-cancer.html (last accessed July 3, 2023).

[12] "Grupo de convencionales se bajan de La Lista del Pueblo y pasan a llamarse «Pueblo Constituyente»" (*El Mostrador*, September 1, 2021). www.elmostrador.cl/dia/2021/09/01/grupo-de-convencionales-se-bajan-de-la-lista-del-pueblo-y-pasan-a-llamarse-pueblo-constituyente/ (last accessed July 4, 2023). "De qué partido son los constituyentes y cómo se distribuyen dentro de la Convención Constitucional" (*BioBio*, February 18, 2022). www.biobiochile.cl/especial/una-constitucion-para-chile/noticias/2022/02/18/a-que-partido-o-lista-pertenece-cada-convencional-constituyente.shtml (last accessed July 4, 2023).

engagement (individual or collective) to understand the impact of new ICTs on political organizations. The PRO shows how ICTs can be used to obviate the need to engage volunteers via groups with territorial or functional reference. This case also shows how individual engagement does not transform individuals into party stakeholders.

The PRO was an early adopter of technology for engaging people in campaigns in the Latin American context. The party was able to organize and mobilize a large number of supporters. However, the individual engagement of supporters through new ICTs reinforced the existing distribution of power within the party. These new supporters were not able to exercise effective voice or to engage in collective action within the party, either to influence decision-making or to compete for office. Atomized supporters did not transform the landscape of the party structures and the decision-making processes.

The PRO is a center-right party in Argentina. Mauricio Macri, a businessman and President between 2015 and 2019, was its founding leader. The party was born during the major economic and political crisis of the early 2000s. The City of Buenos Aires has been its electoral stronghold, and since 2007 it has continually won the mayoralty of the city. In its process of political growth, the PRO incorporated leaders from different backgrounds engendering a more heterogeneous composition of its leadership. The PRO unified different center-right political organizations and expanded its national reach (Vommaro 2017, 2023). Former Peronists, members of the Unión Cívica Radical (Civic Radical Union, UCR) or traditional right-wing politicians, as well as entrepreneurs, CEOs, and leaders from NGOs, joined the party over the years (Morresi and Vommaro 2014). However, Macri and his inner circle maintained control of the brand and party strategy. To become competitive at the national level and expand the electorate beyond Buenos Aires, in 2015 the PRO built an alliance with the UCR and other parties.[13] This electoral alliance, Cambiemos, won the national election in 2015 and Mauricio Macri became President.

The party did not originally pursue a strategy to promote the engagement of supporters using digital communication and data management. The extensive use of volunteers for electoral campaigning was an initiative promoted by two campaign managers, Federico Morales and Guillermo Riera, who brought the idea to the leaders of the party. The former was the person in charge of digital political communication for the PRO, with previous experience in digital communication for the banking sector. The latter, Federico Morales, was a consultant with vast experience in field campaigns in Central America.

---

[13] The alliance also included other minor parties, such as the Coalición Cívica (Civic Coalition, CC) and other niche parties.

When Riera and Morales suggested the idea to the party leaders, the leadership was reluctant to include supporters and eventually activists in the party. The leaders considered that doing so would imply incorporating them into the organizational structure. They had two main concerns. First, the leaders did not want to lose control of the party and, second, the inclusion of new activists in the organization would challenge the local leaders' authority (Federico Morales, PRO, Argentina). Riera's and Morales's proposal broke with the party's conventional strategy for organizational development and candidate recruitment. Cooptation was the traditional means to recruit members and prospective candidates in the PRO. Recruitment, controlled by party leaders, was oriented to incorporate college students mostly from private universities, businessmen and businesswomen, and well-known entertainment and sports figures (Grandinetti 2015; Vommaro 2017).

The strategy to engage volunteers on a large scale in the 2015 national election built on the experience that Riera and Morales developed for the 2013 midterm elections. For those midterm elections they developed a small campaign to recruit volunteers, called Sumate (Join Us). This consisted of an online platform where supporters could sign up to join the campaign. It was available on the party's website, and it was advertised through social networks. They did not have much support from the party or from the campaign. Nonetheless, the Sumate campaign was able to recruit 15,000 people. The success of Riera's and Morales' initiative in 2013, its low costs, and their persistent advocacy helped to convince the PRO leadership to scale up the campaign for the 2015 presidential election. This campaign was called Voluntarios por el Cambio (Volunteers for Change) and it was controlled from the party's headquarters.

Without new ICTs, recruiting a large number of volunteers would have been impossible for a party like PRO, a party with a weak organizational structure without national reach. New ICTs helped the PRO contact and engage supporters, facilitated the administration of data provided by supporters, the delivery of information and campaign propaganda, and the personalized assignment of tasks. This was performed in a centralized and top-down fashion.

In the case of the PRO, the use of new ICTs to engage supporters in the 2015 electoral campaign involved a process of trial and error. The party did not outsource the development of the software and the process of gathering and administering the data. These tasks were performed by a twenty-five-person team of communications and digital mobilization staff. It was led by Marcos Peña (Director of Communications during the 2015 presidential campaign and a prominent member of the party's leading coalition), Riera, and Morales. The team included programmers, communication experts, community managers, designers, people in charge of direct communication via email and instant messaging apps, and people in charge of administering bots for automatic conversation.

The communications and digital mobilization team developed a structured process to contact people, obtain their data, and include them in a systematic process of communication. The campaign engaged these registered supporters in different campaign tasks, such as the distribution of messages and campaign information, and in the process of recruiting more people and identifying supporters by sharing their contacts (Guillermo Riera, PRO, Argentina). The organization in charge of this campaign to recruit and organize supporters was pyramidal. At the top level were a few qualified professionals and party leaders who controlled the entire operation. In a second level were provincial teams. In a third tier were leaders at the municipal level. Finally, under the leader at the municipal level, there were neighborhood supporters. Using an online platform, the team at the top level monitored and controlled the lower levels' work of contacting people. Guillermo Riera summarized how they monitored the evolution of the campaign: "Our [online CRM] tool provides a way to monitor goals. This technological tool receives the data, sets goals, and monitors their fulfillment." (Guillermo Riera, PRO, Argentina).

The campaign to recruit supporters was a great success: The party was able to gather the data and organize over 900,000 volunteers (Federico Morales, PRO, Argentina). Nonetheless, it did not introduce any change to the organizational dynamics of the party and, more critically, it did not change the power dynamics at all (Sol Figueroa, PRO, Argentina). Marcos Peña insisted that their goal was not to build more organizational structure (Federico Morales, PRO, Argentina). Rather, the goal was to achieve electoral success without engendering changes in the party organizational structure. There was variation in how the campaign was implemented in different parts of the territory, but it essentially entailed creating a one-on-one relationship with volunteers. Notwithstanding the success of the campaign, the party organization did not improve its territorial reach, because it was simply not the party leaders' goal and they explicitly rejected it as an option.

Supporters who joined the campaign were not invited to join a group with a territorial reference. As Esteban Bianchi (PRO, Argentina) recalled, gathering supporters in groups was conceived as "old politics." The campaign asked supporters simply to amplify the message, sometimes to organize meetings at home with acquaintances, to participate in campaign rallies and talks, and to provide more contacts to the campaign. Thus, the strategy was oriented to get votes for party candidates and to ask people to persuade prospective voters, essentially using new ICTs. People could gather spontaneously and eventually demand space to participate. However, as Federico Morales (PRO, Argentina) stated, the campaign managers did not initiate or promote such gatherings and did not provide venues and channels for collective engagement.

The campaign collected information and preferences from supporters to improve campaign deployment and communication with prospective voters in field. This campaign strategy involved a controlled interaction (Gerbaudo 2021; Stromer-Galley 2019) with supporters and voters. Federico Morales illustrates this idea as follows:

> The people's main task is to persuade one or two people. This is the way to optimize people's energy. Why? Because, always, when campaigns begin, people show up and want to help. At one point, you ask yourself, what shall I do with all these people? [one person told me] 'I had a plan to modify a bridge [in the area]' 'No, dude, [I told him], I need votes.'

The mobilization of volunteers based on new ICTs had strictly electoral purposes. Thus, the party did not maintain or improve its data infrastructure and its communication with supporters. Guillermo Riera referred to this issue as follows:

> It was extremely hard to convince the party that this had to go on [after the elections], because parties are not prepared for this. The campaign is over, and they tell you 'see you next year.' What 'next year?!' We have to keep working! . . . but no. (Guillermo Riera, PRO, Argentina).

We designed a survey to describe how the party recruits adherents and even activists without incorporating them as party stakeholders. We distributed the survey using the party's mailing list. This database of volunteers was built by the team led by Morales and Riera during the different volunteer recruitment campaigns (Join Us in 2013, Volunteers for Change in 2015, and Defenders of Change in 2019). The database also includes adherents not recruited during these campaigns. The party agreed to distribute a link to our survey to the individuals in this volunteer database. The survey was distributed between June 17, 2021 and July 19, 2021, during an electoral year in Argentina.[14] By the time this survey was distributed, the PRO was starting its electoral campaign. 2,103 recipients clicked on the survey link, of whom 2,083 decided to answer the survey. 1,558 of the invitees who clicked on the survey link declared themselves to be PRO adherents, of whom 1,169 completed the survey. As Jäger (2017) suggests, to improve representativeness, a researcher can use a post-stratification strategy. We post-stratified this sample with the known parameters

---

[14] Midterm legislative elections took place on November 14, 2021. The primaries took place on September 12.

of sex, age, and place of residence drawn from the PRO adherents' database, which the PRO provided.

In accord with the qualitative evidence presented above, 74 percent of the respondents reported that they do not attend meetings of a group of adherents or activists, whether in person or online. This is consistent with the finding that 23 percent of the respondents had participated in an online or in-person meeting in the preceding month. Yet, not participating in meetings does not imply that adherents are disconnected from the party. In fact, 77 percent of our respondents claimed to have received a communication from the PRO frequently or very frequently during electoral campaigns. This proportion remains high even between elections (51 percent). As expected, adherents who lack connection to other adherents are not as committed to party activities as are those who are connected to other adherents. While those who participate in groups report dedicating 14.0 hours a month on average to party activities between elections, and 20.6 hours a month during electoral campaigns, those who do not participate in groups report dedicating 4.5 and 5.5 hours a month between and during elections, respectively. Those who do not participate in organized PRO groups are nonetheless engaged with the party and report dedicating a significant amount of time to party activities. Also, their engagement with the party does not change significantly during and between elections.

The same pattern of commitment is observed in the engagement with instant messaging apps (i.e. WhatsApp and Telegram): 27 percent of respondents report belonging to either a WhatsApp or Telegram group or to a message distribution list. These groups seem to be very active (especially during electoral campaigns); 60 percent of the respondents who belong to a WhatsApp or Telegram group or are part of a distribution list claim that those groups or lists post messages on a daily basis, or several times a week. The most distinctive attribute of these groups is that they are not the online platform of groups that work together offline. People who participate in these groups do not know each other. These groups are not used to organize activities at the local level or to discuss policy positions or PRO's strategy. These groups are essentially tools to disseminate information and propaganda of the party (see Table 2).

The PRO resembles a conventional party with a few activists and many adherents (Duverger 1954; Scarrow 2015; Scarrow, Webb, and Poguntke 2017). New ICTs facilitate communications and contacting supporters. Moreover, new ICTs enable the sporadic activation of supporters to perform campaign tasks individually without convening them in groups. Notwithstanding the massive mobilization of volunteers, the promotion of individual engagement did not alter the conventional picture of a party like the PRO, where only few adherents become activists with high levels of engagement in party life.

**Table 2** Characterization of PRO adherents' WhatsApp and Telegram Groups.

| Group characterization[*] | Percentage |
|---|---|
| Members can interact, but they do not know most of the group members. | 42% |
| Distribution list, members cannot post messages. | 37% |
| The group is used to ask members to disseminate information to contacts and to post content in social networks. | 34% |
| Members can interact and know most of the group members. | 32% |
| The group is used to organize activities at the local level. | 24% |
| The group is used to discuss PRO positions and party strategy. | 17% |

**Source:** Online survey.
[*] How would you characterize the WhatsApp and Telegram groups that you are a member of (select all that apply)?

The case of the PRO illustrates how the use of new ICTs, based on individual engagement, does not necessarily strengthen the party organization nor alter the composition of party stakeholders. For an organization that concentrates power among a party clique and that explicitly seeks to avoid any challenges to the party elite, the incorporation of new ICTs can be a useful way to mobilize supporters. New ICTs do not automatically determine how new volunteers will be engaged. Rather, the strategic decision by PRO leaders to promote individual engagement, that is, limiting opportunities for adherents to participate collectively within the party, prevented the transformation of supporters into party stakeholders. The PRO evolved into a hybrid organization that combines a traditional organizational structure, whereby members play a role in the fulfillment of party functions, with new ICT-enabled platforms that engage party supporters individually to perform campaign tasks.

## Partido Nacional

The introduction of new ICTs in institutionalized parties competes with existing organizational structures and established communication practices to fulfill the functions that such technologies are designed for. As a result, in some cases, because new ICTs cannot replace organizational structures or existing channels of communications, they are not fully used and incorporated as "mundane tools" in the life of the party. In some cases, individuals decide to incorporate new ICTs for their partisan activities by relying on available standard technologies for everyday communications. This precludes the consolidation of specific technological tools designed for the party for similar purposes.

The PN designed an app, +Cerca (Closer) to improve its internal communications and to share information about party activities and contact details of the rank-and-file. This initiative was undertaken in the context of the party's attempt to improve its central structure. The custom-built app did not consolidate as a communications tool among party authorities and members at different levels. The initiative collided with a decentralized party with institutionalized factions and had to compete with standard tools of communication based on new ICTs (e.g. WhatsApp).

The PN was born in 1836 and is among the oldest parties in the world. Pérez Antón (1988) states that its evolution is inescapably intertwined with that of its main rival, the Partido Colorado (Colorado Party, PC). The two parties fought in violent conflicts in the first half of the nineteenth century. Democracy in Uruguay is the result of an agreement between the PC and PN to establish political competition based on free and fair elections. This agreement was guaranteed in the 1918 Constitution (Buquet and Moraes 2018).

The PN has deep roots in the rural sector and in urban centers in the countryside. Organizationally, since its inception, the PN has been a party with institutionalized factions (Buquet, Chasquetti, and Moraes 1998). For most of the twentieth century, the PN, as well as the PC, had two major factions; a conservative and a center-left faction. However, after the birth of the leftist Frente Amplio (Broad Front, FA) in 1971, both parties gradually became more homogeneously center-right parties. After the return of democracy in 1985 following a period of dictatorship, the PN was the governing party between 1990 and 1995 (Luis Alberto Lacalle Herrera was the president) and between 2020 and 2025 (Luis Lacalle Pou was the president). Notwithstanding the party's recent greater ideological homogeneity, it has retained its factionalized and decentralized structure.

The main bodies of the party are the National Convention and the Directorate. The Directorate is the highest executive authority. It comprises a president, three secretaries, and eleven members. The party has a minimal common structure that coordinates between factions. Factions have a dense organizational structure and organize the political actions and the candidate selection and nomination at different levels. The decentralized nature of the daily operation of the party is also manifested in the use of social media. Fernando Benzano (PN, Uruguay) mentioned that by 2014 (a national election year) most of the campaign efforts, including the communication in social networks, were undertaken by each faction. There was an overlap of different communication tools and networks (Beartiz Argimón, PN, Uruguay).

In 2017, the party introduced the app +Cerca (Closer). The party was trying to improve its internal institutional communications, the quality of information it had about its members, and the levels of affiliation with the party (Felipe Paullier; Fernando Benzano; and Jhonatan De Vecchi, PN, Uruguay). The creation of the app +Cerca was conceived as part of a broader process of building a central database of party members, especially of those who hold office at different levels of government.

The PN paid close attention to the experience of the PRO in Argentina. According to Fernando Benzano:

> The PN had no experience in communications, no strategy, especially regarding communication in social networks. They [the PRO] had invested in forging a database, data collection, social listening, it was impressive ( . . . ) that is how we decided to implement a CRM here [in the PN]. (Fernando Benzano, PN, Uruguay)

Around 2014, the national authorities of the party initiated a process to reinforce the central structures of the party. Among different measures, the party developed a strategy to build a formal central party membership database. In this regard, the incorporation of new ICTs implied the effort to build a unified database of leaders and active members across the country. The party lacked such a unified database. The strategy to enlarge the database was to require individuals to register as a party member in order to participate in different party events. For example, members of the party had to be registered to use the app +Cerca. The collection of information to build the database was a labor-intensive effort that took eighteen months. By the end of the process the party had a database of approximately 4,000 members, leaders, and activists (Fernando Benzano, PN, Uruguay). The party invested in a CRM to manage the database.

The initial efforts to introduce new ICTs in party activities had some positive results for the organization of common political action. For example, in the 2014 primary election in Montevideo and, subsequently, in the national election that same year, the party developed a tool to distribute poll watchers to report vote counts to a centralized system. According to Jhonatan De Vecchi, the successful implementation of this technology paved the way for the initiative of the national directorate to develop the app +Cerca. It also informed the general assessment that the party had to improve and modernize its internal communications strategy. Fernando Benzano recalled "everyone was demanding" to improve the party's internal communications (Fernando Benzano, PN, Uruguay).

The main functions of the app for users were the availability of party members' contact details and the ability to promote party activities. Fernando Benzano (PN, Uruguay) summarizes the main political motivation of the app as follows:

> For us, adherence to the party was important, because we started to have more information; with increasing levels of adherence, the database expanded. At one point there was the idea that new adherents could have access to the app, though only leaders (from any level, though) would have access to the list of contacts (Fernando Benzano, PN, Uruguay).

The developers of the app +Cerca nonetheless faced the reluctance of the local leaders of different factions who did not want to share their lists of contacts (Gonzalo Baroni, PN, Uruguay). These leaders opposed the distribution of such information because they considered this information a political asset, a key resource for their internal electoral competition: "It is very hard, even today, to persuade factions to give you their databases. We have decided to go our own way, to generate our own databases, without touching those of the factions ( . . . ) It all depends on resources and unfortunately the party has not invested in this." (Fernando Benzano, PN, Uruguay).

The app never replaced existing networks or means of communication. According to Gonzalo Baroni (PN, Uruguay), +Cerca was a good idea, but it never fully materialized. The app was not a channel for leaders to communicate with each other. It was essentially used to find news of the party in the press (the app provided press clippings). Communications between leaders from different levels was channeled through the instant messaging app, WhatsApp. Interviewees agreed that the party youth do not use it. The initiative was not sustained over time and it is now inactive. The case of the PN illustrates an unsuccessful attempt to incorporate new ICTs. The push to incorporate this tool encountered resistance from local party leaders and factions. Moreover, the rank-and-file did not see any advantage to the new custom app compared to the more general ICTs (i.e. WhatsApp) that they were already using for their daily operations. Therefore, the attempt to incorporate new ICTs did not produce an empowered or a hybrid organization.

## Frente Amplio

The decision to introduce new ICTs in institutionalized parties potentially raises tensions and conflict. These technologies might be seen by intermediate bodies and the rank-and-file as a challenge to their practices, their place, and their role in the organization. This especially occurs in parties that have a dense organization and engaged activists. Tensions arise when technology is conceived by party leaders as a substitute for people in fulfilling party functions. When these technologies fail to be presented as tools to empower people it is more likely that they will fail to become widely used mundane tools in the organization. These new technologies remain limited to those more inclined to incorporate them (e.g. youth). The problems derived from the technological readiness (or lack thereof) of the rank-and-file and the grassroots activists interact with their disinclination to consent to the incorporation and to pay the opportunity cost of learning new tools and introducing new practices.

The presidents of the FA sought to introduce different technological tools to incorporate new FA supporters to the party debates. First, in 2017, Javier Miranda, then president of the party, introduced FAro (Lighthouse). It was a discussion forum platform to enable exchanges among FA supporters. Second, also in 2017, Miranda presented Quilt, a software tool to manage adherents' information and integrate data from different public sources. Finally, in 2023, during the presidency of Fernando Pereira, the FA introduced the tool Nexo (Nexus), which is a software tool that is similar to Quilt, but which is oriented to help grassroots local groups (Base Committees) communicate with adherents and manage their database of information about adherents.

The FA was formed in 1971 as a coalition of leftist parties and splinter factions from the two traditional parties (PN and PC). Since its inception, the coalition has received the support of a movement of self-organized grassroots activists. This initial composition gradually became institutionalized in a party with a dual structure: a grassroots structure and a coalitional structure. Both structures share power in party decision-making in each of the three levels of the party: the grassroots level, the intermediate level, and the national level. The interplay between grassroots activists and factions engenders checks and balances and diffuse power distribution within the party (Pérez Bentancur, Piñeiro Rodríguez, and Rosenblatt 2020). Therefore, leaders are not only permanently accountable to the rank-and-file but also must negotiate with grassroots activists and factions or preemptively consider their preferences.

The party has a complex organizational structure, with several collective decision-making structures. The highest directive body of the FA is the National Plenary. It comprises 170 delegates. Factions and grassroots activists have the same number of delegates. All delegates are elected in open internal elections with secret voting. The National Political Board is the permanent executive body. It comprises the president and vice president of the party, fifteen representatives from the FA factions and eleven delegates from the grassroots activists. The latter are organized in base committees that convene FA adherents with a territorial or functional reference, for example, adherents who reside in the same area or work in the same sector, respectively. The FA has around 470 base committees throughout the country.[15] A base committee can be described as a modest locale furnished with basic facilities. Volunteer grassroots activists sustain the functioning of base committees. In base committees, FA grassroots activists come together to engage in discussions about local, national, or global politics. They also serve as a conduit for grassroots activists' voice to the FA's decision-making bodies and coordinate the electoral campaigns in the field. A substantial presence of grassroots activists permeates every level of the party's structure, including its highest decision-making bodies.

In 2011, the National Plenary of the FA decided to form a commission to generate a proposal to incorporate online participation in the FA statutes. As with every ad hoc commission, task force, or formal body of the FA, this commission was formed by grassroots activists and FA faction leaders. In August 2012, the commission presented its conclusions to the National Plenary. The commissions considered it necessary to incorporate new online participatory tools to attract new members as activists, especially young adherents. However, it also specified that these new tools could not substitute for offline participation. Moreover, adherents who joined the party had to be linked to a base committee. Regardless of the nature of the prospective online communication tool, the party members using it must have at least one offline meeting to validate the online group and its decisions. The administrators of online groups fulfill not a technical but a political role and had to be appointed by the pertinent FA body.[16]

In April 2017, the president of the FA, Javier Miranda, invited all FA adherents to join a new online participatory platform, called FAro.[17] In this invitation, Miranda outlined the goals and functionalities of the online platform. Adherents could register on the platform to participate in online forums structured by topics. Also, adherents could propose new forums about new topics. The goal was to incorporate in party discussions not only those party adherents who were already participating in offline party meetings but also those who were not participating in offline organizational bodies. Finally, members of in-person party branches at the neighborhood level could create their own online forums. The discussion in the forums could feed the decision-making process. For example, the president of the FA claimed that there were going to be forums

---

[15] "Día del Comité de Base del FA" (*UYPress*, August 26, 2023). www.uypress.net/Politica/Pereira–La-gente-ha-dejado-de-creer-en-este-gobierno-le-ha-perdido-la-confianza–uc131236 (last accessed August 28, 2023).

[16] Resolution, Plenario Nacional (National Plenary), August 5, 2012.

[17] "Convocatoria: FAro – un espacio de participación frenteamplista" (*Communication of the FA Presidency*, April 10, 2017).

in the FAro to discuss a draft document on political the strategy for the upcoming electoral campaign.

The development of FAro did not incorporate the grassroots structure perspectives and it did not consider the resolution of the National Plenary of 2012 about online participation. Therefore, it aroused criticism and distrust among the grassroot activists. For example, a grassroots leader said the following in an in-depth interview:

> One day we found that it was a platform [FAro] that was already working. We were informed about its characteristics ( . . . ) What is the real function? ( . . . ) It is a platform that is outside the structure; how is it going to be organically integrated into the structure? What may arise from that network? It is not a minor fact, but also if there are going to be moderators; who are going to be the moderators? What will be their attributions? Will they have the capacity to make a synthesis of the proposals? All these types of things need to be discussed beforehand. In addition, I believe that a negative element may be incurred if we start taking steps in a certain direction, trying to modernize the FA with the new technologies, without having a clear idea of what we want from these new technologies, what it is that we are looking for with them. So, lacking a strategy regarding these new technologies, we can take serious false steps, and they also cost money, because they are certainly not free.

The FAro was a failure. It was not used by adherents or grassroots activists.

In 2017, the FA presidency also introduced the software tool Quilt to integrate data both from party databases (e.g. data about party members) and public sources (e.g. electoral data at district level and census data). This software was developed in Spain, by Dialoga Consultores and it aims to provide information for decision-making processes during electoral cycles.[18] The acquisition of the software was contested by the grassroots delegates from Montevideo at the National Political Board. The grassroots delegates from Montevideo prepared a report enumerating the pros and cons of incorporating this technology and the attributes that they deemed necessary for a tool like this one to be useful and secure for the organization (e.g. the document mentioned that the software had to be open source). The report also called on the FA to have an internal political discussion about the incorporation of new ICTs.[19] Nonetheless, the Mesa Política Nacional (National Political Board) decided to acquire the software.[20] The implementation of the software was not carried out by FA members who usually take care of IT issues, but by technicians from outside the party.

---

[18] The 2014 presidential campaign of Tabaré Vázquez (FA leader) used this software.

[19] Report prepared by the Montevideo Base Committees' Delegates to the Mesa Política Nacional (National Political Board).

[20] Resolution, Mesa Política Nacional, June 16, 2017.

The software was implemented to support the work of the Unidad Estratégica (Strategic Unit) of the party, which provides information for the presidency in the strategic decision-making of the party. This software can be used both for developing capacities at the local level – e.g. the base committees could access the party's database – and for improving the information available at the central level. Yet, the incorporation of the software was only aimed at extracting granular information useful for the decision-making of the party's presidency.[21] Therefore, there was not a consistent strategy to incorporate the software for the daily operations of the grassroots structure. The incorporation was unsuccessful since it was not widely used by the party, especially by the grassroots structure. Moreover, the incorporation of Quilt was not helpful in improving the quality of the party's database, which was viewed within the FA as a priority. In 2023, Quilt was replaced by a new open-source software, Nexo, developed for free by a team of programmers who are FA activists and supporters.

In contrast to Quilt, Nexo was born in response to an initiative from the Comisión Nacional de Organización (National Commission of Organization, CNO), which oversees the political administration and development of the organizational structure. The CNO believed new ICTs could assist the daily operations of the organization in general, and of the grassroots structure in particular. Nexo was developed in close connection with the party's organizational structure, particularly the CNO. Nexo is intended first and foremost to improve and update the party's database. Also, and relatedly, Nexo is meant to help base committees improve their capacities to manage the FA adherents in their territory and to contact and to incorporate new members. Manuel Ferrer, the National Secretary of Organization of the FA, stated in an interview: "We are now aiming to have a party's database tailored to the needs of each base committee." Ferrer later in the interview added: "we need the base committees to take ownership of their databases because that boosts the party, and that can also boost their political activism" (Manuel Ferrer, FA, Uruguay). Nexo has been operational since June 5, 2023. The first major trial for Nexo occurred on the Day of the Base Committee (which is celebrated every August 25th).[22] According to Ferrer, more than 75 percent of the base committees (over 300 base committees)[23]

---

[21] "FA se mete en las redes y enfrenta dilema ético por el uso de datos" (*El Observador*, June 26, 2017), www.elobservador.com.uy/nota/fa-se-mete-en-las-redes-y-enfrenta-dilema-etico-por-el-uso-de-datos-2017626500 (last accessed August 21, 2023).

[22] On that day, every Base Committee holds an assembly to elect its board. This is a celebratory occasion when grassroots activists organize activities in the neighborhood and the activists bring some food and beverages to share with participants. National political leaders and elected representatives visit different Base Committees.

[23] This number far exceeds the number of base committees that used Quilt.

uploaded their information (e.g. list of adherents that participated in the assembly) to Nexo on that day. Manuel Ferrer concluded that:

> In two months [by August], [Nexo] was incorporated by three quarters of the organization and it currently [by the end of September] reaches almost 100% of the organization. We believe this is a political organizational success. It speaks about the goals, [it shows] that the technical team rose to the occasion. They developed a tool that was adapted to the needs of the party, and hence the party perceives it as a tool of its own. It is also [the result of] the interaction [during its development], which gave clarity to the [different actors within the] organization, for example, by explaining [how this tool would work]. (Manuel Ferrer, FA, Uruguay).

The contrast between the experience with Quilt and with Nexo illustrates the difficulties top-down initiatives face incorporating new ICTs in densely organized parties. The initial success of Nexo seems attributable to the engagement of grassroots activists in the process of developing of the tool and to the fact that Nexo was designed to address the needs of activists in their fieldwork. Beyond the problems associated with technological readiness, the successful incorporation of a technological tool is more likely when the party rank-and-file perceive that the new ICT is empowering them. In this case, the latest (successful) attempt to incorporate new ICTs engendered an empowered organization. While we do not aim here to explain this outcome, it seems plausible that the FA's organizational density and complexity, the timing of ICT incorporation, and the characteristics of those who were engaged in its development are significant causal factors.

## Conclusions

Technology has transformed social and political interactions by reducing the cost of information and communication. Technological innovations have significantly lowered the costs of contacting and engaging people with politics. However, new ICTs have not only changed how politicians communicate with citizens but also have transformed how people pursue collective action. Technology affects both the way people join and participate in political organizations. New ICTs allow people to individually engage with parties, without the need to coordinate with others in a structured organization. Yet, to fully assess the effect of new ICTs, we must analyze how they are used by party organizations to engage members in collective action.

Technology can have a dual effect on people within organizations. It can either empower people by giving them the tools they need to organize more efficiently and to increase their leverage in the party's internal political process, or it can disempower people by replacing the need for organizers and intermediate structures. When technology empowers people, it leads to greater democratic responsiveness, as party leaders become more accountable to their members and stakeholders. However, technology can also be used to disempower people and reduce their capacity to hold leaders accountable. People can now more readily engage in electoral campaigns. However, the eventual erosion of traditional organizational structures that support sustained collective action might dilute people's voice within party organizations. Therefore, the effects of technological innovation on people's power within party organizations cannot be fully understood without considering how parties use such technologies to engage people in political activities.

Many factors explain when and how parties incorporate technology (Gibson 2020). The characteristics of a party's electorate and the electoral competition, the affordability of technology, the institutional setting, leaders' preferences, and the attributes of existing organizational structures all influence when and how parties incorporate new ICTs. In our framework, the process of incorporating new ICTs in party organizations comprises two steps. The first step is exogenous, and it explains party leaders' decision of whether to incorporate new ICTs. It essentially depends on factors that are exogenous to party organizations and are associated with the party electorate, the competitive pressures, the affordability of technology, and the campaign regulations. The second step is an endogenous process that defines how parties incorporate new ICTs. This process is shaped by the party's internal dynamics. Party leaders decide whether to introduce new ICTs. However, their level of autonomy to control this process vis-à-vis the party rank-and-file determines the extent and the effects of the incorporation of new ICTs.

In parties where leaders face a weak organization – or even when they face no organization at all, leaders have the capacity to adopt new ICTs to substitute technology for people in performing party functions. In such situations, the adoption of new ICTs is thus only limited by exogenous factors (and interest on the part of leaders), as in the case of Rodolfo Hernández's campaign in Colombia. New ICTs offer the opportunity to engender a low-cost ersatz organization, avoiding the need to invest in a traditional organizational structure.

In contrast, when leaders face a strong organization, party rank-and-file and grassroots leaders might contest when and how to adopt new ICTs, as in the case of the FA in Uruguay and the PRO in Argentina. In this setting, the incorporation of new ICTs might engender a hybrid or an empowered organization. In the former, there is a coexistence between conventional organizational structures and new ICTs' enabled platforms to fulfill three main party functions (recruitment, information, and mobilization) which, in turn, results in a partial substitution of the role of people in the organization (as in the case of the PRO). In the latter, the incorporation of new ICTs improves the capacity of the rank-and-file to fulfill these three main functions (as in the case of the FA). The cases of the PN and the FA in Uruguay show how the incorporation of new ICTs is a conflictive process that can undermine the attempt to incorporate new ICTs or it can engender, simultaneously, both substitution and empowerment of people within the organization.

Many parties in Latin America face difficulties acting as agents of democratic representation and have weak organizational structures. The incorporation of new ICTs obviates the need for leaders to develop an organization to recruit and horizontally coordinate prospective candidates and to contact and mobilize voters. However, new ICTs in and of themselves cannot reproduce the functions performed by traditional organizations. Therefore, when ICTs replace the role people played in party organizations, they engender ersatz organizations. The cases of the LdP in Chile and the presidential campaign of Rodolfo Hernández in Colombia show the possibilities and the limitations of new ICTs for replacing people in organizing complex and sustained collective action. New ICTs grant emerging political actors the opportunity to easily build an electoral vehicle. The case of Rodolfo Hernández in Colombia shows how new ICTs grant the possibility of contacting and grouping many supporters. Yet, they do not by themselves replace the need for investing in organizers to manage supporters in the field to engender complex collective actions in campaigns. The LdP in Chile shows how new ICTs allow for rapid coordination for an electoral campaign, among disperse local leaders, to achieve electoral success. Yet, new ICTs do not provide the necessary tools (rules and socialization) to aggregate preferences, coordinate political actions, and solve conflicts once in office.

New ICTs have brought people back to electoral campaigns. While in the US the revival of people's engagement in campaigns using new ICTs is supported by previously developed party organizations (Nielsen 2012), in Latin America, where weak organizations are pervasive, this engagement is not supported by intermediate party bodies. The intersection between the incorporation of new ICTs and weak party organizations intensifies two effects of new ICTs on political engagement. The first effect is an individual engagement that does not transform citizens engaged in campaigns into political actors, because their involvement is developed in an atomized, rather than a collective or relational, environment. The case of the PRO in Argentina illustrates how new ICTs can engage supporters in campaigns without making them party stakeholders. We label this phenomenon "individual engagement," which allows leaders to engage supporters without risking leaders' power. Second, the lack of intermediate bodies and the concomitant absence of organizers with the capacity to organize people in the field limits the potential of people to develop complex collective action in campaigns, as we showed for the case of Rodolfo Hernández in Colombia.

The technological and political context set the stage for political entrepreneurs to be electorally viable. In dire contexts with daunting challenges and limited resources to campaign, the organization of people, whenever possible, is a requisite and even the only way to achieve electoral success. Conversely, in a favorable context with access to resources to campaign, politicians are released from the need to build a structure to organize people to achieve political relevance. As suggested by Levitsky, Loxton, and Van Dyck (2016) and Van Dyck (2021), favorable context (i.e. access to state resources and mass media) for electoral success prevented parties and leaders from investing in building organizations in Third Wave democracies in Latin America. Broad access to mass media and other state resources makes party organization unnecessary for electoral success. New ICTs also provided a shortcut to the expensive, tedious, and long-term process of building a party organization to contact and engage prospective supporters. While the combination of the expansion of TV and democratization enabled candidates to become electorally successful without developing a political organization in the early 1990s, the new ICTs that emerged in the 2000s engender the possibility of engaging people without organizing them.

In the last quarter of the twentieth century, the mass adoption of TV engendered a Broadcast Political Communication Order (Epstein 2018) and supplanted the role of people in communicating and mobilizing for electoral campaigns (Nielsen 2012). Armies of activists in the field were a complex-to-manage tool that was no longer required to spread the word. In the nascent Information Political Communication Order new ICTs, in turn, have significantly reduced the costs of reaching people, have made it possible to leverage information and intelligence to increase the effectiveness of canvassing, and have enabled massive individual engagement (without the cost of enlarging the stakeholders of the organization). These changes make new ICTs an attractive tool for politicians to engage supporters in campaigns not only because doing so is less expensive than building a traditional party organization, but also because individual engagement does not enlarge the number of party stakeholders and, in turn, the number of potential challengers to party leaders.

The Broadcast Political Communication Order (Epstein 2018) diminished the importance of people in campaigns (Nielsen 2012). Some may claim that new ICTs, as tools for engaging people in campaigns, promote and develop participation within parties. However, the possibility of massive individual engagement, in fact, prevents organizational development or even dilutes the power of organizers and local leaders in parties (Gibson 2020). In this setting, the revival of participation in campaigns does not necessarily entail the revival of participation in politics; whether the latter occurs depends on how technology is incorporated.

The concentration of power within parties implies the exercise of control over the main functions of the organization. In this vein, as leaders increase control over party functions, they reduce other party members' roles in fulfilling such functions. Therefore, party activists become less essential and lose power vis-à-vis the party leadership. New ICTs provide leaders with the opportunity to increase their hold over critical party functions. Leaders can increase their control over the recruitment and selection of candidates, reduce their reliance upon activists to collect information at the local level about citizens' concerns and preferences, and diminish the organization's role in electoral mobilization by individually engaging adherents or sympathizers in campaigns without making them part of the organization.

Ceteris paribus, leaders prefer to concentrate power in their own hands and avoid the development of the organizational structure and the activation of members who could eventually challenge their authority or hold them accountable. While, in our theory, leaders' preferences are constant – they prefer to reduce people's power to hold them accountable – the organizational structure varies across parties. The potential conflict between leaders and the party rank-and-file, in turn, yields different ways of incorporating new ICTs and different outcomes in terms of concentration or distribution of power. In this respect, the incorporation of new ICTs opens a window of opportunity to change the status quo of power distribution within the party organization. In a context of weak party organizations, new ICTs enable leaders to concentrate power while increasing the number of people engaged in campaigns, as in the cases of the PRO in Argentina and Rodolfo Hernández's presidential campaign in Colombia. Therefore, we cannot assume that engaging people in campaigns suffice to incorporate them in the political process. New ICTs foster the illusion that the former intrinsically involves the latter. The cases reviewed in this Element suggest otherwise. Mobilization without political incorporation may engender greater distrust among citizens toward parties and increase the latter's difficulties in fulfilling their political representation function in democracies.

# References

Aldrich, John. 1995. *Why Parties?: The Origin and Transformation of Political Parties in America*. Chicago: University of Chicago Press.

Aldrich, John, Rachel Gibson, Marta Cantijoch, and Tobias Konitzer. 2016. "Getting Out the Vote in the Social Media Era: Are Digital Tools Changing the Extent, Nature and Impact of Party Contacting in Elections?" *Party Politics* 22 (2): 165–178.

Anria, Santiago, Verónica Pérez Bentancur, Rafael Piñeiro Rodríguez, and Fernando Rosenblatt. 2022. "Agents of Representation: The Organic Connection between Society and Leftist Parties in Bolivia and Uruguay." *Politics & Society* 50 (3): 384–412.

Baldwin-Philippi, Jessica. 2015. *Using Technology, Building Democracy: Digital Campaigning and the Construction of Citizenship*. New York: Oxford University Press.

Barberà, Oscar, Giulia Sandri, Patricia Correa, and Juan Rodríguez-Teruel. 2021. "Political Parties Transition into the Digital Era." In *Digital Parties: The Challenges of Online Organisation and Participation*, edited by Oscar Barberà, Giulia Sandri, Patricia Correa, and Juan Rodríguez-Teruel, 1–22. Cham: Springer International.

Bastos dos Santos, João Guilherme, Miguel Freitas, Alessandra Aldé, Karina Santos, and Vanessa Cristine Cardozo Cunha. 2019. "WhatsApp, política mobile e desinformação: a hidra nas eleições presidenciais de 2018." *Comunicação & Sociedade* 41 (2): 307–334.

Bene, Marton. 2017. "Go Viral on the Facebook! Interactions between Candidates and Followers on Facebook during the Hungarian General Election Campaign of 2014." *Information, Communication & Society* 20 (4): 513–529.

Benkler, Yochai, Robert Faris, and Hal Roberts. 2018. *Network Propaganda: Manipulation, Disinformation, and Radicalization in American Politics*. New York: Oxford University Press.

Bennett, W. Lance, and Alexandra Segerberg. 2013. *The Logic of Connective Action: Digital Media and the Personalization of Contentious Politics*. New York: Cambridge University Press.

Bennett, W. Lance, and Steven Livingston. 2020. *The Disinformation Age: Politics, Technology, and Disruptive Communication in the United States*. New York: Cambridge University Press.

Biancalana, Cecilia, and Davide Vittori. 2021. "Cyber-Parties' Membership between Empowerment and Pseudo-participation: The Cases of Podemos and the Five Star Movement." In *Digital Parties: The Challenges of Online Organisation and Participation*, edited by Oscar Barberà, Giulia Sandri, Patricia Correa, and Juan Rodríguez-Teruel, 109–126. Cham: Springer International.

2023. "Business as Usual? How Gamification Transforms Internal Party Democracy." *The Information Society* 39 (5): 282–295. https://doi.org/ 10.1080/01972243.2023.2241470. https://doi.org/10.1080/01972243 .2023.2241470.

Bimber, Bruce. 2003. *Information and American Democracy: Technology in the Evolution of Political Power*. New York: Cambridge University Press.

Bimber, Bruce, Andrew Flanagin, and Cynthia Stohl. 2012. *Collective Action in Organizations*. New York: Cambridge University Press.

Bogliaccini, Juan Ariel, Ignacio Borba, Cecilia Giambruno, Martín Opertti, and Rafael Piñeiro Rodríguez. 2019. *Twittarquía: La Política de las Redes en Uruguay*. Montevideo: Túnel – Universidad Católica del Uruguay.

Bond, Becky, and Zack Exley. 2016. *Rules for Revolutionaries: How Big Organizing Can Change Everything*. White River Junction: Chelsea Green.

Brinks, Daniel M., Steven Levitsky, and Maria Victoria Murillo. 2020. *Understanding Institutional Weakness: Power and Design in Latin American Institutions*. New York: Cambridge University Press.

Buquet, Daniel, Daniel Chasquetti, and Juan Andrés Moraes. 1998. *Fragmentación Política y Gobierno en Uruguay: ¿Un Enfermo Imaginario?* Montevideo: Facultad de Ciencias Sociales.

Buquet, Daniel, and Juan Andrés Moraes. 2018. "Construyendo un Equilibrio Democrático: La Reforma Constitucional de Uruguay en 1917." *Revista Uruguaya de Ciencia Política* 27 (1): 19–39.

Carrillo, Arturo J., and Matías Jackson. 2022. "Follow the Leader? A Comparative Law Study of the EU's General Data Protection Regulation's Impact in Latin America." *Vienna Journal on International Constitutional Law* 16 (2): 177–262.

Chadwick, Andrew. 2017. *The Hybrid Media System: Politics and Power*. New York: Oxford University Press.

Corredor, Paola. 2022. "El Éxito y el Fracaso de la Campaña Presidencial de Rodolfo Hernández." Licenciatura en Ciencia Política, Departamento de Ciencia Política, Universidad de los Andes.

Cox, Gary W. 1997. *Making Votes Count: Strategic Coordination in the World's Electoral Systems: Political Economy of Institutions and Decisions*. Cambridge: Cambridge University Press.

Dalton, Russell, Ian McAllister, and Martin Wattenberg. 2000. "The Consequences of Partisan Dealignment." In *Parties without Partisans: Political Change in*

*Advanced Industrial Democracies*, edited by Russell Dalton and Martin Wattenberg, 37–63. Oxford: Oxford University Press.

Dalton, Russell, and Martin Wattenberg, eds. 2000. *Parties without Partisans: Political Change in Advanced Industrial Democracies*. Oxford: University Press Oxford.

Dalton, Russell, and Steven Weldon. 2007. "Partisanship and Party System Institutionalization." *Party Politics* 13 (2): 179–196.

Davis, Stuart, and Joe Straubhaar. 2020. "Producing Antipetismo: Media Activism and the Rise of the Radical, Nationalist Right in Contemporary Brazil." *International Communication Gazette* 82 (1): 82–100.

De Blasio, Emiliana, and Lorenzo Viviani. 2020. "Platform Party between Digital Activism and Hyper-Leadership: The Reshaping of the Public Sphere." 8 (4): 16–17. https://doi.org/10.17645/mac.v8i4.3230. www.cogitatiopress.com/mediaandcommunication/article/view/3230.

Dommett, Katharine. 2020. "Roadblocks to Interactive Digital Adoption? Elite Perspectives of Party Practices in the United Kingdom." *Party Politics* 26 (2): 165–175. https://doi.org/10.1177/1354068818761196. https://journals.sagepub.com/doi/abs/10.1177/1354068818761196.

Downs, Anthony. 1957. *An Economic Theory of Democracy*. New York: Harper and Row.

Duverger, Maurice. 1954. *Political Parties*. London: Methuen.

Enli, Gunn Sara, and Eli Skogerbø. 2013. "Personalized Campaigns in Party-Centred Politics: Twitter and Facebook as Arenas for Political Communication." *Information, Communication & Society* 16 (5): 757–774.

Epstein, Ben. 2018. *The Only Constant Is Change: Technology, Political Communication, and Innovation over Time*. New York: Oxford University Press.

Evangelista, Rafael, and Fernanda Bruno. 2019. "WhatsApp and Political Instability in Brazil: Targeted Messages and Political Radicalisation." *Internet Policy Review* 8 (4): 1–23.

Gainous, Jason, and Kevin M. Wagner. 2014. *Tweeting to Power: The Social Media Revolution in American Politics*. New York: Oxford University Press.

Ganz, Marshall. 2009. *Why David Sometimes Wins: Leadership, Organization, and Strategy in the California Farm Worker Movement*. New York: Oxford University Press.

George, Alexander L., and Andrew Bennett. 2005. *Case Studies and Theory Development in the Social Sciences*. Cambridge, MA: MIT Press.

Gerbaudo, Paolo. 2021. "Are Digital Parties More Democratic than Traditional Parties? Evaluating Podemos and Movimento 5 Stelle's Online Decision-Making Platforms." *Party Politics* 27 (4): 730–742.

Gibson, Rachel. 2015. "Party Change, Social Media and the Rise of 'Citizen-Initiated' Campaigning." *Party politics* 21 (2): 183–197.

———. 2020. *When the Nerds Go Marching in: How Digital Technology Moved from the Margins to the Mainstream of Political Campaigns*. New york: Oxford University Press.

Gibson, Rachel, Fabienne Greffet, and Marta Cantijoch. 2017. "Friend or Foe? Digital Technologies and the Changing Nature of Party Membership." *Political Communication* 34 (1): 89–111. https://doi.org/10.1080/10584609.2016.1221011. https://doi.org/10.1080/10584609.2016.1221011.

Gomez, Raul, and Luis Ramiro. 2019. "The Limits of Organizational Innovation and Multi-Speed Membership: Podemos and Its New Forms of Party Membership." *Party Politics* 25 (4): 534–546. https://doi.org/10.1177/1354068817742844. https://journals.sagepub.com/doi/abs/10.1177/1354068817742844.

González-Cacheda, Bruno, and Celso Cancela Outeda. 2024. "Digitalisation and Political Parties in Europe." *Party Politics* 0 (0): 13540688231225639. https://doi.org/10.1177/13540688231225639. https://journals.sagepub.com/doi/abs/10.1177/13540688231225639.

Grandinetti, Juan. 2015. "'Mirar para Adelante': Tres Dimensiones de la Juventud en la Militancia de Jóvenes PRO." In *Hagamos Equipo: PRO y la Construcción de la Nueva Derecha en Argentina*, edited by Gabiel Vommaro and Sergio Morresi, 231–263. Los Polvorines: Ediciones UNGS.

Guess, Andrew M., and Benjamin A. Lyons. 2020. "Misinformation, Disinformation, and Online Propaganda." In *Social Media and Democracy: The State of the Field, Prospects for Reform*, edited by Nathaniel Persily and Joshua Tucker, 10–33. New York: Cambridge University Press.

Han, Hahrie. 2014. *How Organizations Develop Activists: Civic Associations and Leadership in the 21st Century*. New York: Oxford University Press.

Hazan, Reuven, and Gideon Rahat. 2010. *Democracy within Parties: Candidate Selection Methods and Their Political Consequences*. Oxford: Oxford University Press.

Hersh, Eitan D. 2015. *Hacking the Electorate: How Campaigns Perceive Voters*. New York: Cambridge University Press.

Invernizzi-Accetti, Carlo, and Fabio Wolkenstein. 2017. "The Crisis of Party Democracy, Cognitive Mobilization, and the Case for Making Parties More Deliberative." *American Political Science Review* 111 (1): 97–109.

Issenberg, Sasha. 2012. *The Victory Lab: The Secret Science of Winning Campaigns*. New York: Broadway Books.

Jacobs, Kristof, and Niels Spierings. 2019. "A Populist Paradise? Examining Populists' Twitter Adoption and Use." *Information, Communication & Society* 22 (12): 1681–1696.

Jäger, Kai. 2017. "The Potential of Online Sampling for Studying Political Activists Around the World and across Time." *Political Analysis* 25 (3): 1–15.

Karpf, David. 2012. *The MoveOn Effect: The Unexpected Transformation of American Political Advocacy*. New York: Oxford University Press.

2016. *Analytic Activism: Digital Listening and the New Political Strategy*. New York: Oxford University Press.

Katz, Richard, and Peter Mair, eds. 1994. *How Parties Organize: Change and Adaptation in Party Organizations in Western Democracies*. London: Sage.

Kitschelt, Herbert, Kirk Hawkins, Juan Pablo Luna, Guillermo Rosas, and Elizabeth Zechmeister. 2010. *Latin American Party Systems*. New York: Cambridge University Press.

Kreiss, Daniel. 2012. *Taking Our Country Back: The Crafting of Networked Politics from Howard Dean to Barack Obama*. New York: Oxford University Press.

2016. *Prototype Politics: Technology-Intensive Campaigning and the Data of Democracy*. New York: Oxford University Press.

Kreiss, Daniel, and Adam J. Saffer. 2017. "Networks and Innovation in the Production of Communication: Explaining Innovations in U.S. Electoral Campaigning from 2004 to 2012." *Journal of Communication* 67 (4): 521–544.

Larrain, Guillermo, Gabriel Negretto, and Stefan Voigt. 2023. "How Not to Write a Constitution: Lessons from Chile." *Public Choice* 194 (3–4): 233–247.

Levitsky, Steven, James Loxton, and Brandon Van Dyck. 2016. "Introduction." In *Challenges of Party-Building in Latin America*, edited by Steven Levitsky, James Loxton, Brandon Van Dyck, and Jorge Domínguez, 1–48. New York: Cambridge University Press.

Luna, Juan Pablo. 2014. *Segmented Representation: Political Party Strategies in Unequal Democracies*. Oxford: Oxford University Press.

Luna, Juan Pablo, Cristian Pérez, Sergio Toro, et al. 2022. "Much Ado about Facebook? Evidence from 80 Congressional Campaigns in Chile." *Journal of Information Technology & Politics* 19 (2): 129–139. https://doi.org/10.1080/19331681.2021.1936334.

Luna, Juan Pablo, Rafael Piñeiro Rodríguez, Fernando Rosenblatt, and Gabriel Vommaro. 2021. *Diminished Parties: Democratic Representation in Contemporary Latin America*. New York: Cambridge University Press.

Machado, Caio, Beatriz Kira, Vidya Narayanan, Bence Kollanyi, and Philip Howard. 2019. "A Study of Misinformation in WhatsApp Groups with a Focus on the Brazilian Presidential Elections." Companion Proceedings of the 2019 World Wide Web Conference, San Francisco, USA.

Mainwaring, Scott, ed. 2018. *Party Systems in Latin America: Institutionalization, Decay, and Collapse*. New York: Cambridge University Press.

Mainwaring, Scott, and Edurne Zoco. 2007. "Political Sequences and the Stabilization of Interparty Competition." *Party Politics* 13 (2): 155–178.

McAlevey, Jane. 2016. *No Shortcuts: Organizing for Power in the New Gilded Age*. New York: Oxford University Press.

McKenna, Elizabeth, and Hahrie Han. 2014. *Groundbreakers: How Obama's 2.2 Million Volunteers Transformed Campaigning in America*. New York: Oxford University Press.

Morresi, Sergio, and Gabriel Vommaro. 2014. "Argentina: The Difficulties of the Partisan Right and the Case of Propuesta Republicana." In *The Resilience of the Latin American Right*, edited by Juan Pablo Luna and Cristóbal Rovira Kaltwasser, 319–342. Baltimore: Johns Hopkins University Press.

Nielsen, Rasmus Kleis. 2011. "Mundane Internet Tools, Mobilizing Practices, and the Coproduction of Citizenship in Political Campaigns." *New Media & Society* 13 (5): 755–771.

2012. *Ground Wars: Personalized Communication in Political Campaigns*. Princeton: Princeton University Press.

Nocetto, Lihuen, Verónica Pérez Bentancur, Rafael Piñeiro Rodríguez, and Fernando Rosenblatt. 2021. "Unorganized Politics. The Political Aftermath of the Social Unrest in Chile." America Political Science Association, Seattle, Washington, September 30–October 3.

Panebianco, Angelo. 1988. *Political Parties: Organization and Power*. New York: Cambridge University Press.

Parasuraman, A. 2000. "Technology Readiness Index (Tri): A Multiple-Item Scale to Measure Readiness to Embrace New Technologies." *Journal of Service Research* 2 (4): 307–320.

Pérez Antón, Romeo. 1988. "Cuatro Antagonismos Sucesivos: La Concreta Instauración de la Democracia Uruguaya." *Revista de Ciencia Política* (2), 41–59.

Pérez Bentancur, Verónica, Rafael Piñeiro Rodríguez, and Fernando Rosenblatt. 2020. *How Party Activism Survives: Uruguay's Frente Amplio*. New York: Cambridge University Press.

Piaia, Victor, and Marcelo Alves. 2020. "Abrindo a caixa preta: análise exploratória da rede bolsonarista no WhatsApp." *Intercom: Revista Brasileira de Ciências da Comunicação* 43: 135–154.

Raniolo, Francesco, Valeria Tarditi, and Davide Vittori. 2021. "Political Parties and New ICTs: Between Tradition and Innovation." In *Digital Parties: The Challenges of Online Organisation and Participation*, edited by Oscar Barberà, Giulia Sandri, Patricia Correa, and Juan Rodríguez-Teruel, 181–204. Cham: Springer International.

Resende, Gustavo, Philipe Melo, Hugo Sousa, et al. 2019. "(Mis) Information Dissemination in WhatsApp: Gathering, Analyzing and Countermeasures." The World Wide Web Conference, San Francisco, May 13–17.

Rights, Office of the High Commissioner for Human. 2021. *The Right to Privacy in the Digital Age: Report (2021)*. United Nations. www.ohchr .org/en/calls-for-input/2021/right-privacy-digital-age-report-2021.

Roberts, Kenneth. 2014. *Changing Course in Latin America: Party Systems in the Neoliberal Era*. New York: Cambridge University Press.

Robinson, Laura, Jeremy Schulz, Matías Dodel, et al. 2020. "Digital Inclusion across the Americas and Caribbean." *Social Inclusion* 8 (2): 244–259.

Römmele, Andrea. 2003. "Political Parties, Party Communication and New Information and Communication Technologies." *Party Politics* 9 (1): 7–20.

Sartori, Giovanni. 1976. *Parties and Party Systems: A Framework for Analysis*. New York: Cambridge University Press.

Scarrow, Susan. 2015. *Beyond Party Members: Changing Approaches to Partisan Mobilization*. Oxford: Oxford University Press.

Scarrow, Susan, Paul Webb, and Thomas Poguntke. 2017. *Organizing Political Parties: Representation, Participation, and Power*. Oxford: Oxford University Press.

Schmuck, Desirée, and Michael Hameleers. 2020. "Closer to the People: A Comparative Content Analysis of Populist Communication on Social Networking Sites in pre-and post-Election Periods." *Information, Communication & Society* 23 (10): 1531–1548.

Siavelis, Peter M., and Scott Morgenstern, eds. 2008. *Pathways to Power: Political Recruitment and Candidate Selection in Latin America*. University Park: Pennsylvania State University Press.

Stinchcombe, Arthur. 1968. *Constructing Social Theories*. New York: Harcourt, Brace & World.

Stromer-Galley, Jennifer. 2019. *Presidential Campaigning in the Internet Age.* 2nd ed. New York: Oxford University Press.

Treré, Emiliano. 2020. "The Banality of WhatsApp: On the Everyday Politics of Backstage Activism in Mexico and Spain." *First Monday* 25 (12).

Tsebelis, George. 1995. "Decision Making in Political Systems: Veto Players in Presidentialism, Parliamentarism, Multicameralism and Multipartyism." *British Journal of Political Science* 25 (3): 289–325.

Tufekci, Zeynep. 2017. *Twitter and Tear Gas: The Power and Fragility of Networked Protest.* New Haven: Yale University Press.

Vaccari, Cristian, and Augusto Valeriani. 2016. "Party Campaigners or Citizen Campaigners? How Social Media Deepen and Broaden Party-Related Engagement." *The International Journal of Press/Politics* 21 (3): 294–312.

Van Dyck, Brandon. 2017. "The Paradox of Adversity: The Contrasting Fates of Latin America's New Left Parties." *Comparative Politics* 49 (2): 169–192.

2021. *Democracy against Parties: The Divergent Fates of Latin America's New Left Contenders.* Pittsburgh: University of Pittsburgh Press.

Vommaro, Gabriel. 2017. *La Larga Marcha de Cambiemos.* Buenos Aires: Siglo XXI Editores.

2023. *Conservatives against the Tide: The Rise of the Argentine PRO in Comparative Perspective.* Cambridge: Cambridge University Press.

# Cambridge Elements ≡

# Politics and Society in Latin America

## Maria Victoria Murillo

*Columbia University*

Maria Victoria Murillo is Professor of Political Science and International Affairs at Columbia University. She is the author of Political Competition, Partisanship, and Policymaking in the Reform of Latin American Public Utilities (Cambridge, 2009). She is also editor of Carreras Magisteriales, Desempeño Educativo y Sindicatos de Maestros en América Latina (2003), and co-editor of *Argentine Democracy: The Politics of Institutional Weakness* (2005). She has published in edited volumes as well as in the *American Journal of Political Science, World Politics*, and *Comparative Political Studies*, among others.

## Juan Pablo Luna

*The Pontifical Catholic University of Chile*

Juan Pablo Luna is Professor of Political Science at Pontificia Universidad Católica de Chile. He received his BA in Applied Social Sciences from the UCUDAL (Uruguay) and his PhD in Political Science from the University of North Carolina at Chapel Hill. He is the author of *Segmented Representation. Political Party Strategies in Unequal Democracies* (Oxford University Press, 2014), and has co-authored *Latin American Party Systems* (Cambridge University Press, 2010). In 2014, along with Cristobal Rovira, he co-edited *The Resilience of the Latin American Right* (Johns Hopkins University). His work on political representation, state capacity, and organized crime has appeared in the following journals: *Comparative Political Studies, Revista de Ciencia Política, the Journal of Latin American Studies, Latin American Politics and Society, Studies in Comparative International Development, Política y Gobierno, Democratization, Perfiles Latinoamericanos*, and the *Journal of Democracy*.

## Andrew Schrank

*Brown University*

Andrew Schrank is the Olive C. Watson Professor of Sociology and International & Public Affairs at Brown University. His articles on business, labor, and the state in Latin America have appeared in the *American Journal of Sociology, Comparative Politics, Comparative Political Studies, Latin American Politics & Society, Social Forces*, and *World Development*, among other journals, and his co-authored book, *Root-Cause Regulation: Labor Inspection in Europe and the Americas*, is forthcoming at Harvard University Press.

Alfred P. Montero, *Carlton College*
Alison Post, *University of California, Berkeley*
Gabriel Vommaro, *Universidad Nacional de General Sarmiento*
Deborah Yashar, *Princeton University*
Gisela Zaremberg, *Flacso México*
Veronica Zubilaga, *Universidad Simon Bolivar*

## About the Series

Latin American politics and society are at a crossroads, simultaneously confronting serious challenges and remarkable opportunities that are likely to be shaped by formal institutions and informal practices alike. The Elements series on Politics and Society in Latin America offers multidisciplinary and methodologically pluralist contributions on the most important topics and problems confronted by the region.

# Cambridge Elements ≡

## Politics and Society in Latin America

### Elements in the Series

A full series listing is available at: www.cambridge.org/PSLT

Printed in the United States
by Baker & Taylor Publisher Services